Caregiver Substance Use and Child Trauma

Research has consistently shown that there is a link between caregiver substance use and child maltreatment, but less attention has been given to child trauma exposure. The co-occurrence of caregiver substance misuse and child trauma exposure is a prevailing problem that has confounded social work prevention, protection, and treatment efforts with both children and adults for years. However, there has been minimal empirical and clinical literature focusing on child trauma as an outcome of caregiver substance use. This work is designed to be the catalyst for sustained intellectual inquiry about how caregiver substance use, child maltreatment, and violence exposure can be understood in theory and practice. To this end, the research presented in this book highlights the state of the science, the impact of the phenomenon, and the policy and practice questions that must be addressed. Implications for social work practice are highlighted in order to attenuate these deleterious and pervasive problems in the future.

This book was originally published as a special issue of the *Journal of Social Work Practice in the Addictions*.

Michele Staton-Tindall, Ph.D., is an Associate Professor in the University of Kentucky, USA, at the College of Social Work and a Faculty Associate of the university's Center on Trauma and Children and Center on Drug and Alcohol Research. Her research interests include evidence-based substance abuse treatment, service utilization, and rural populations.

Ginny Sprang, Ph.D., is a Professor in the College of Medicine, Department of Psychiatry and Executive Director of the University of Kentucky Center on Trauma and Children, USA. Dr. Sprang has published extensively in leading journals focusing on violence, maltreatment, and traumatic stress in families, children and professionals.

Shulamith Lala Straussner, DSW., is Professor at the New York University Silver School of Social Work, USA, and Director of the Post-Master's Certificate Program in Clinical Approaches to Addiction. She is also Editor of the *Journal of Social Work Practice in the Addictions*.

Caregiver Substance Use and Child Trauma

Implications for Social Work Research and Practice

Edited by
Michele Staton-Tindall, Ginny Sprang and
Shulamith Lala Straussner

LONDON AND NEW YORK

First published 2014
by Routledge
2 Park Square, Milton Park, Abingdon, Oxon, OX14 4RN

Simultaneously published in the USA and Canada
by Routledge
711 Third Avenue, New York, NY 10017

Routledge is an imprint of the Taylor & Francis Group, an informa business

British Library Cataloguing in Publication Data
A catalogue record for this book is available from the British Library

ISBN13: 978-0-415-71063-3

Typeset in Garamond
by Taylor & Francis Books

Publisher's Note
The publisher accepts responsibility for any inconsistencies that may have arisen during the conversion of this book from journal articles to book chapters, namely the possible inclusion of journal terminology.

Disclaimer
Every effort has been made to contact copyright holders for their permission to reprint material in this book. The publishers would be grateful to hear from any copyright holder who is not here acknowledged and will undertake to rectify any errors or omissions in future editions of this book.

Contents

Citation Information

The following chapters were originally published in the *Journal of Social Work Practice in the Addictions*, volume 13, issue 1 (January-March 2013). When citing this material, please use the original page numbering for each article, as follows:

Chapter 1
Caregiver Substance Use and Child Outcomes: A Systematic Review
Michele Staton-Tindall, Ginny Sprang, James Clark, Robert Walker and Carlton D. Craig
Journal of Social Work Practice in the Addictions, volume 13, issue 1 (January-March 2013) pp. 6-31

Chapter 2
Family Structure, Substance Use, and Child Protective Services Involvement: Exploring Child Outcomes and Services
Natasha Mendoza
Journal of Social Work Practice in the Addictions, volume 13, issue 1 (January-March 2013) pp. 32-49

Chapter 3
Puerto Rican Parenting and Acculturation in Families Experiencing Substance Use and Intimate Partner Violence
Cristina Mogro-Wilson, Lirio K. Negroni and Michie N. Hesselbrock
Journal of Social Work Practice in the Addictions, volume 13, issue 1 (January-March 2013) pp. 50-69

Chapter 4
Caregiver Substance Abuse and Children's Exposure to Violence in a Nationally Representative Child Welfare Sample
Kristen D. Seay and Patricia L. Kohl
Journal of Social Work Practice in the Addictions, volume 13, issue 1 (January-March 2013) pp. 70-90

Chapter 5
Advancing Trauma-Informed Systems Change in a Family Drug Treatment Court Context
Laurie A. Drabble, Shelby Jones and Vivian Brown
Journal of Social Work Practice in the Addictions, volume 13, issue 1 (January-March 2013) pp. 91-113

Chapter 6

African American Adult Children of Alcoholics: An Interview With J. Camille Hall, PhD, LCSW
Interview Conducted by Lori Holleran Steiker
Journal of Social Work Practice in the Addictions, volume 13, issue 1 (January-March 2013) pp. 118-122

Endpage

Mentalization-Based Treatment: A Valuable Framework for Helping Maltreating Parents
Christine H. Fewell
Journal of Social Work Practice in the Addictions, volume 13, issue 1 (January-March 2013) pp. 123-126

Notes on Contributors

Vivian Brown, Founder and Former CEO, PROTOTYPES Centers for Innovation in Health, Mental Health and Social Services, Manhattan Beach, California, USA

James Clark, Professor, School of Social Work, University of Cincinnati, Cincinnati, Ohio, USA

Carlton D. Craig, Associate Professor, College of Social Work, University of Kentucky, Lexington, Kentucky, USA

Laurie A. Drabble, Professor, School of Social Work, San Jose State University, San Jose, California, USA

Christine H. Fewell, Adjunct Professor, Silver School of Social Work, New York University, New York, USA

Michie N. Hesselbrock, Emeritus Professor, School of Social Work, University of Connecticut, West Hartford, USA

Lori Holleran Steiker, Associate Professor, School of Social Work, University of Texas at Austin, Texas, USA

Shelby Jones, Graduate Research Assistant, School of Social Work, San Jose State University, California, USA

Patricia L. Kohl, Associate Professor, Brown School of Social Work, Washington University in St. Louis, Missouri, USA

Natasha Mendoza, Assistant Professor of Social Work, College of Public Programs, Arizona State University, Phoenix, Arizona, USA

Cristina Mogro-Wilson, Assistant Professor, School of Social Work, University of Connecticut, West Hartford, USA

Lirio K. Negroni, Associate Professor, School of Social Work, University of Connecticut, West Hartford, Connecticut, USA

Kristen D. Seay, Doctoral Candidate, Brown School of Social Work, Washington University in St. Louis, St. Louis, Missouri, USA

Ginny Sprang, Professor, University of Kentucky College of Medicine, USA

Michele Staton-Tindall, Associate Professor, University of Kentucky College of Social Work, USA

Shulamith Lala Straussner, Professor, New York University Silver School of Social Work, USA

Robert Walker, Assistant Professor, College of Social Work, University of Kentucky, Lexington, Kentucky, USA

Introduction

MICHELE STATON-TINDALL, GINNY SPRANG AND SHULAMITH LALA STRAUSSNER

Research has consistently shown that there is a link between caregiver substance use and child maltreatment (Drapela & Mosher, 2007; Dube, et al., 2001; Kelleher, Chaffin, Hollenberg, & Fischer, 1994; Magura & Laudet, 1996; Suchman, Rounsaville, DeCoste, & Luthar, 2007; Sprang, Clark, & Staton-Tindall, 2010; Staton-Tindall, Sprang, & Clark, 2012; Yampolskaya & Banks, 2006). Of particular interest to social workers, one longitudinal analysis examining reasons for re-referrals to Child Protective Services (CPS) found that children whose caregivers abused substances were significantly more likely to be re-reported for child maltreatment, and those claims were more likely to be substantiated (Fluke et al., 2008). The Adverse Childhood Experiences (ACE) study found that individuals who grew up in households where the parents abused substances experienced nearly four lifetime adverse childhood experiences compared to 1.4 events among those whose parents did not abuse substances (Dube et al., 2001). Negative consequences of caregiver alcohol and drug use may be due to such familial dynamics as "communication problems, conflict, chaos and unpredictability, inconsistent messages to children, breakdown in rituals and traditional family rules and boundaries, and emotional, physical and, at times, sexual abuse" (Straussner, 2011, p. 5). In addition, the life style associated with caregiver illicit drug use is often characterized by illegal activities, a series of live-in partners and incarcerations, as well as high risk for HIV and other serious medical problems, all of which tend to have a severe negative impact on the children.

While the existing research consistently documents the deleterious consequences of caregiver substance use for children, little work has examined the impact through the lens of ***trauma***. Empirical trauma research reveals that infants and children are often traumatized when they are exposed to events that directly threaten their well-being or the health and welfare of those they love (Christopher, 2004; Scheeringa & Gaensbauer, 2000). Traumatic events experienced by children whose caregivers use substances – including accidents, unintentional injuries, and caregiver-inflicted harm – are common. For example, Maxson et al. (2009) found that among a sample of *pediatric trauma patients*, about a third of their caregivers engaged in risky or hazardous levels of alcohol use. This prevalence rate is considerably higher than 16% of caregivers who acknowledged alcohol or drug use in a primary pediatric clinic (Lane et al., 2007).

Trauma exposure experienced by children of substance-involved caregivers is frequently generated by interpersonal violence within the family, producing powerful, long-term impressions on the child's sense of self and potentially impacting their basis for future relationships (Ciccheti & Toth, 2000). The consequences for children of prolonged trauma exposure can include chronic guilt, helplessness and terror, which in turn, may increase their sense of powerlessness and vulnerability, risk for re-victimization and/or identification with the perpetrator, as well as substance use later in life. In other words, adult psychological structures can be profoundly shaped by childhood trauma exposure and by a child's responses to these events (Herman, 1992; James, 1994). Moreover, more recent research by Perry (2009) and Zeanah (2009) suggest that the impact of a stressful environment on the neurological development of children can serve as a primary indicator for later health, mental health, and socio-behavioral consequences. Thus, caregiver substance use can have a powerful influence on a child's development, and subsequently on their responsiveness to treatment.

While the co-occurrence of caregiver substance misuse and child trauma exposure is a prevailing problem that has confounded prevention, protection and treatment efforts with both children and adults for years, there has been minimal empirical and clinical literature focusing on child trauma as an outcome of caregiver substance use (Sprang et al., 2010; Staton-Tindall et al., 2012). This work is designed to be the catalyst for sustained intellectual inquiry about how caregiver substance use, child maltreatment, and violence exposure can be understood in theory and practice. To this end, this collection highlights the state of the science, the impact of the phenomenon, and the policy and practice questions that must be addressed. Implications for social work practice are highlighted in order to attenuate these deleterious and pervasive problems in the future.

This book begins with a systematic review that examines how well the extant literature synthesizes and builds upon findings from the child maltreatment and substance use fields to address the impact of caregiver substance use and trauma exposure. Noting a silo effect in how relevant literature has developed over time, Dr. Staton-Tindall and colleagues discuss differences in perspectives between child protective interests and adult substance abuse treatment and rehabilitation efforts, and how the current state of the science in measurement and research design contribute such silo effects. The authors note the paucity of research that bridges the gap between these two perspectives, and how integrated interventions that address caregiver substance misuse and safe and effective parenting might advance the policy and practice agendas in both areas.

One method of such integration involves the infusion of trauma-informed perspectives into systems of care that serve children and substance-using adults. A key aspect of any trauma-informed approach is implementing proper procedures for identifying children at risk for exposure to traumatic events. Mendoza and colleagues, and Mogro-Wilson, Negroni & Hesselbrock provide insights into the treatment needs of these complexly troubled families, by documenting the impact of caregiver substance misuse on family acculturation, victimization and structure, parenting, and child well-being outcomes. Understanding how families organize themselves to create risk or protection for their children, and how these youth respond to different types of parental and family functioning provides insights into how to tailor appropriate interventions. A study by Seay and Kohl presents one of the first examinations of the relationship between substance abuse and children's exposure to violence in a large, diverse, and nationally representative sample of child-welfare involved families. This study outlines specific predictors of child exposure to violence (direct or through witnessing), and, as such, provides a risk profile of vulnerable children and families that should be targeted for comprehensive trauma assessments.

Drabble, Jones & Brown examine the implementation of a trauma framework and trauma-specific services into family drug court. This investigation is particularly relevant as this is the arena where a wide variety of players (e.g. the judiciary, child welfare, mental health, addiction science) come together to address the needs of families where substance misuse and child trauma co-occur. The utilization of a trauma-informed approach to guide the work of an interdisciplinary team is an exemplar of how to structure integrated, trauma-informed treatments for caregiver substance misuse and child traumatic stress.

This collection also includes an interview with Dr. J. Camille Hall – a prominent researcher who has devoted a significant amount of work to understanding the experiences of adult African American children of alcoholics – particularly the role of ethnicity and culture. A review of a book focusing on impact of substance abuse on children and a brief discussion of two videos that can help educate social work students to the dynamics of growing up with a substance-abusing parent are included. The work concludes with an Endnote discussion of mentalization-based treatment, a promising new intervention for helping those in substance abuse treatment become better parents.

This book highlights how the field of social work is uniquely qualified to respond to the policy and practice challenges presented by the complexities associated with substance use within families. Social work as a discipline emphasizes cross-systems collaborations and the integration of interdisciplinary knowledge to benefit the most vulnerable populations. It is therefore paramount that we harness the collective interest and expertise of the social work profession towards the dissolution of silos that make it difficult for cross-fertilization and collaboration among the fields of addiction science, traumatic stress, child welfare and children's mental health.

REFERENCES

Christopher, M. (2004). A broader view of trauma: A biopsychosocial-evolutionary view of the role of the traumatic stress response in the emergence of pathology or growth. Clinical Psychology Review, 24, 75–98.

Ciccheti, D., & Toth, S. L. (2000). Developmental processes in maltreated children. Nebraska Symposium on Motivation, 46, 85–160.

Drapela, L. A., & Mosher, C. (2007). The conditional effect of *parental drug use* on *parental* attachment and adolescent *drug use*: Social control and social development model perspectives. Journal of Child & Adolescent Substance Abuse, 16, 63-87.

Dube, S. R., Anda, R. F., Felitti, V. J., Croft, J. B., Edwards, V. J., & Giles, W. H. (2001). Growing up with parental alcohol abuse: exposure to childhood abuse, neglect, and household dysfunction. Child Abuse Neglect, 25, 1627–1640.

Fluke, J. D., Shusterman, G. R., Hollinshead, D. M., & Yuan, Y. Y. (2008). Longitudinal analysis of repeated child abuse reporting and victimization: Multistate analysis of associated factors. Child Maltreatment, 13(1), 76–88.

Herman, J. (1992). Complex PTSD: A syndrome in survivors of prolonged and repeated trauma. Journal of Traumatic Stress, 5, 377–391.

James, B. (1994). Handbook for treatment of attachment-trauma problems in children. New York: Maxwell Macmillan International.

Kelleher, K., Chaffin, M., Hollenberg, J., & Fischer, E. (1994). Alcohol and drug disorders among physically abusive and neglectful parents in a community-based sample. American Journal of Public Health, 84, 1586–1590.

Lane, W. G., Dubowitz, H., Feigelman, S., Kim, J., Prescott, L., Meyer, W., & Tracy, J. K. (2007). Screening for parental substance abuse in pediatric primary care. Ambulatory Pediatrics, 7(6), 458–462.

Magura, S., & Laudet, A. B. (1996). Parental substance abuse and child maltreatment: Review and implications for intervention. Children and Youth Services Review, 18, 193–220.

Maxson, R. T., Yuma-Guerroero, P., von Sternberg, K., Lawson, K. A., Johnson, K. M., Brown, J., Smith, C., & Velasquez, M. M. (2009). Screening for risky alcohol use among caregivers of pediatric trauma patients: A pilot study. Journal of Trauma, 67(1 Supplement), S37–S42.

Perry, B. D. (2009). Examining child maltreatment through a neurodevelopmental lens: clinical applications of the neurosequential model of therapeutics. Journal of Loss and Trauma, 14(4), 240–255.

Scheeringa, M. S., & Gaensbauer, T. J. (2005). Posttraumatic Stress Disorder. In C. H. Zeanah (Ed.), Handbook of infant mental health (2nd ed.): The Guilford Press.

Sprang, G., Clark, J. J., & Staton-Tindall, M. (2010). Caregiver substance use and trauma exposure in young children. Families in Society, 91(4), 401–407. DOI: 10.1606/1044-3894.4029.

Staton-Tindall, M., Sprang, G., & Clark, J. (2012). Caregiver drug use and arrest as correlates of child trauma exposure. Journal of Evidence-Based Social Work, 9(3), 265–282. DOI: 10.1080/15433714.2010.494982.

Straussner, S.L.A. (2011). Children of substance abusing parents: An overview. In Straussner, S.L.A. & Fewell, C. H. (Eds). Children of Substance Abusing Parents: Treatment Issues and Interventions (1–27). NY: Springer Press

Suchman, N. E., Rounsaville, B., DeCoste, C., & Luthar, S. (2007). Parental control, parental warmth, and psychosocial adjustment in a sample of substance-abusing mothers and their school-aged and adolescent children. Journal of Substance Abuse Treatment, 32, 1–10.

Yampolskaya, S., & Banks, S. M. (2006). An assessment of the extent of child maltreatment using administrative databases. Assessment, 13(3), 342–355.

Zeanah, C. H. (2009). The importance of early experiences: Clinical, research, and policy perspectives. Journal of Loss and Trauma, 14(4), 266–279.

Caregiver Substance Use and Child Outcomes: A Systematic Review

MICHELE STATON-TINDALL, PhD
Associate Professor, College of Social Work, University of Kentucky, Lexington, Kentucky, USA

GINNY SPRANG, PhD
Professor, College of Medicine, University of Kentucky, Lexington, Kentucky, USA

JAMES CLARK, PhD
Professor, School of Social Work, University of Cincinnati, Cincinnati, Ohio, USA

ROBERT WALKER, MSW, LCSW
Assistant Professor, College of Social Work, University of Kentucky, Lexington, Kentucky, USA

CARLTON D. CRAIG, PhD
Associate Professor, College of Social Work, University of Kentucky, Lexington, Kentucky, USA

In spite of widespread concern that children living with substance-misusing caregivers are experiencing greater risk for maltreatment, little research examines the direct effects of caregiver substance use on child outcomes. This systematic review investigates the work done within and across disciplines of adult substance abuse, child welfare, and child mental health, including the measurement of key terms, conceptualization of primary variables, and suggested implications for translational science to practice. The findings of the review show considerable shortcomings for examining this complex problem. To move research forward, we suggest ways to improve measures and methods to provide more robust support for inferences about child maltreatment and mental health outcomes.

The National Center on Addiction and Substance Abuse (CASA) estimates that about 50% of U.S. children live with a caregiver who uses alcohol, illicit substances, or tobacco (CASA, 2005). Tobacco is the most common substance used in many of these homes (approximately 27 million), but an estimated 17 million children are exposed to caregivers engaging in binge drinking, and 9.2 children million have caregivers using illicit substances (CASA, 2005). The Substance Abuse and Mental Health Services Administration (SAMHSA) recently reported that more than 8 million children between 2002 and 2007 lived with at least one caregiver who abused alcohol or used illicit substances during the past year or was dependent on those substances (National Survey on Drug Use and Health [NSDUH], 2009).

The relationship between caregiver substance misuse and child maltreatment has been the target of research in the clinical and empirical literature for many years (Dunn et al., 2002; Johnson & Leff, 1999; Magura & Laudet, 1996; Testa & Smith, 2009; Wells, 2009). A number of reasons have been offered for why substance misuse adversely affects children. The abuse of substances can diminish caregivers' ability to respond to children's cues for nurturing, and can impair judgment of priorities related to care, supervision, and guidance (Testa & Smith, 2009). Caregiver involvement with drug-using lifestyles often leads to unstable and chaotic home environments for children and can even involve exposure to crime or toxic substances. Caregiver substance misuse can also seriously affect caregiver expression of emotion, which can interfere with secure caregiver–child attachments. These problems then can lead to negative consequences for children's development of emotional regulation, confidence, social skills, and trustful relationships with others (Department of Health and Human Services [DHHS], 2009). Research indicates that these children disproportionately suffer from other mental health, behavioral, and academic problems (DHHS, 2009). Caregiver substance misuse has also been documented as a powerful predictor of severity of maltreatment of children (Sprang, Clark, & Bass, 2005).

In addition, caregiver substance misuse is among the most powerful and robust predictors of children developing addiction disorders as adolescents (e.g., Widom, White, Czaja, & Marmorstein, 2007), and this suggests that substance use among adolescents is a coping strategy to deal with their chaotic and violent family lives (Kilpatrick, Acierno, Saunders, Resnick, & Best, 2000). Such adolescents are more likely to become involved with the criminal justice system (Huebner & Gustafson, 2007; Murray, Janson, & Farrington, 2007).

Given the findings about the effects of caregiver substance misuse on children, research that concurrently examines these effects from both the caregiver and child perspective is very limited. Typically, the research has either examined maltreatment among children with some consideration for caregiver substance misuse, or it has been focused on adult substance abuse, with peripheral examination of parenting behaviors. Thus, one body of literature has taken a child protective interest as it examines caregiver substance misuse (Johnson & Leff, 1999; Kroll, 2004). Another very large body of research has looked at adult substance misuse patterns and the interests and needs of these individuals for treatment and rehabilitation (Magura & Laudet, 1996; Testa & Smith, 2009). The difference in perspectives between child protective interests and adult rehabilitation mirrors the tension in public policy between goals of child protection versus family reunification. These dual foci are often at odds in cases when both cannot be satisfied and one interest must predominate. Thus far, the literature has done little to bridge the gap between these two perspectives by examining how integrated treatment (for substance misuse and parenting) or other interventions might serve both goals. These distinct research perspectives have yielded important information for the substance misuse and child maltreatment fields, but they pose challenges to practitioners and policymakers when converting scientific information into either policy or practice. It is reasonable to speculate that the relationships among these phenomena are not simple and universal across all caregiver–child configurations, and that their effects will vary for different children living in various contexts.

The purpose of this article is to review relatively current literature that examined caregiver substance misuse as it impacts or influences child maltreatment with consideration for the specificity of substance use measures, child maltreatment measures, and the degree to which studies could link caregiver substance use with child outcomes. Essentially, the question revolved around how well the emerging literature steps outside the two research silos of child maltreatment and substance abuse.

To explore this problem, a review was conducted to examine relevant, empirical work that has been accomplished within and across disciplines of adult substance misuse, child welfare, and child mental health. The objectives were to include literature that (a) examined measurement of caregiver substance use as an independent variable, (b) examined child maltreatment as a dependent variable, and (c) examined the implications of the existing research for addressing this problem.

METHOD

Systematic Literature Review and Analysis

This review was based on literature searches of peer-reviewed articles in scholarly databases. One primary search engine was Academic Search Premier (ASP), which enabled searches in Medline, PsychINFO, and Social

Work Abstracts. Given the medical implications of substance misuse and child maltreatment, PubMed (PM) was also utilized. Primary search terms with the initial number of displayed articles for those terms in parentheses were caregiver substance use and child maltreatment (7 articles ASP, 9 articles PM), caregiver substance use and child neglect (3 articles ASP, 31 articles PM), caregiver substance use and child abuse (10 articles ASP, 30 articles PM), parental substance use and child neglect (22 articles ASP, 332 articles PM), and parental substance use and child abuse (60 articles ASP, 331 articles PM). Given the large body of research on child trauma in relation to caregiver behavior, we also included "caregiver substance use and child trauma" in the search terms, but curiously, this only yielded four articles across both search engines (ASP and PM). One of the articles was repeated under the other search terms, and the other three articles did not meet search criteria for the study. Therefore, for consistency and clarity of operationalization, the primary dependent variable search term focused on issues related to child maltreatment rather than child trauma.

From the initial display of articles for each of these terms, final articles were selected for systematic review based on meeting the targeted criteria for this review based on the following decision rules:

1. Articles had to be empirical, data-driven studies (no literature reviews or meta-analyses).
2. Parental or caregiver substance use must have been used as an independent variable. For example, articles that included substance use as a covariant or mediating variable were not included in this analysis.
3. The primary dependent variable for the study must have focused on the child—including any form of child maltreatment such as neglect or abuse, accidental injury, or behavioral or psychological outcome.
4. The analytic approach was intended to examine the relationship between caregiver substance use and child outcomes.
5. Articles with a publication date since 2000 were included to garner the most recent approaches in measurement and the most current thinking in implications for practice and research.

Twenty-three articles met the inclusion requirement for this study. A content analysis approach was used to address each of the primary objectives of the article. For Objective 1, the articles were organized to define measurement of key constructs, including substance misuse, child outcomes, and potential covariants used in the analysis. Other key elements of the sample were also outlined for descriptive purposes. For Objective 2, the articles were organized by their outcome relative to child maltreatment, including (a) acts of maltreatment (physical abuse, sexual abuse, neglect, and frequency and severity of harm) or (b) other child outcomes (any and all emotional, cognitive, or behavioral response, typically to either a maltreatment event or response to caregiver substance misuse), and primary findings were described. The table was then reorganized so that child maltreatment outcomes were grouped together and other child outcomes were together to easily compare study findings. For Objective 3, discussion sections of each article were carefully examined and organized into tabular format and compared for their implications for particular types of professions. To show the practice relevance for findings, we identified potential user groups broadly into child welfare, child mental health, or adult caregiver substance misuse professions.

RESULTS

Complexity of Measurement

Caregiver substance misuse

As shown in Table 1, some articles used standardized and widely used substance use assessment tools such as the Addiction Severity Index (Connors-Burrow, Johnson, & Whiteside-Mansell, 2009; Van de Mark et al., 2005), Composite International Diagnostic Interview Short Form (Barth, Gibbons, & Guo, 2006), Michigan Alcohol Screening Test (Jester, Jacobson, Sokol, Tuttle, & Jacobson, 2000; Ondersma, 2002), and the Timeline FollowBack Method (Jester et al., 2000). These tools allowed for assessment of a number of variables to determine indicators of problem severity associated with alcohol or illicit substance use. Using either these or other tools, a few articles examined their primary measure of substance use in terms of frequency of drug and alcohol use (Bailey, Hill, Oesterle, & Hawkins, 2009; Berger, 2005). Although these articles reflect consistency with the overall substance use literature in assessment of problem severity and frequency of use, they were limited in comparison to the larger body of literature on adult substance misuse independent of relationship to child care or maltreatment. The majority of articles in this review included only a single item indictor of "any substance use," and the primary method of data collection included secondary analysis from child protective service (CPS) records. Other measures to note included perceptions of caregiver substance misuse by the child or adolescent or the CPS worker. Thus across these studies, validated and extensive self-reports, brief self-reports, investigation records, and provider and professional opinions were used, making across-study comparisons impossible.

Child maltreatment

Measures of child maltreatment were more clearly defined. Standardized tools such as the Child Behavior Checklist (CBCL; Achenbach, 1991) were commonly used to measure parent's report of child internalizing behavior and child externalizing behavior (Bailey et al., 2009; McNichol & Tash, 2001;

TABLE 1 Measurement Summary of Substance Use and Child Outcome Variables

Author	Child Sample	Caregiver Sample	Substance Use Measurement	Child Outcome Measurement
Bailey et al. (2009)	808 students, ages 10–16	Parents of elementary school children	Frequency of alcohol, marijuana, and cigarette use	CBCL (parent externalizing behavior, child externalizing behavior), parental monitoring, harsh discipline, IPV
Barth et al. (2006)	1,101 children in the NSCAW data set	Female caregivers with at least one indicator of substance abuse treatment need	Active alcohol or drug problem, need for substance abuse treatment, positive screen on CIDI-SF	Based on CPS report, was a rereport of abuse or neglect filed within 18 months of original case
Berger (2005)	2,760 families	Population-based telephone survey respondents	Number of times using drugs or being drunk in the past year	Violence against children: Conflict Tactic Scale, other physical abuse
Connors-Burrow et al. (2009)	70 children enrolled in substance abuse treatment with mother	55 mothers in substance abuse treatment	Addiction Severity Index	Frequency of exposure to violence (TSH scale)
Crandall et al. (2006)	3,808 mother–child dyads	Biological mothers 1 year postpartum	Self-reported use of any alcohol or illicit drugs	Sustained an injury requiring medical attention during the first year of life
DiLauro (2004)	261 children, ages 1 month to 17 years	Any parent or caregiver	Based on CPS records, any use of alcohol and other drugs	Based on CPS records, type of perpetrator maltreatment inflicted (neglect, abuse)
Forrester (2000)	95 children in CPR (CPS)	Primary caregiver of child on the CPR in the target district in London	Based on CPR, case worker perception of parent substance use and areas of "concern"	Category of CPR report: neglect, physical abuse, sexual abuse, emotional abuse
Gibbs et al. (2008)	N/A	3,959 caregiver/soldier with a documented child maltreatment incident	Based on Army Central Registry records, any alcohol or drug use by the child maltreatment offender	Each abuse/neglect type (physical, emotional, or sexual) coded as mild, moderate, or severe

(*Continued*)

TABLE 1 (Continued)

Author	Child Sample	Caregiver Sample	Substance Use Measurement	Child Outcome Measurement
Hanson et al. (2006)	4 023 adolescents, ages 12–17	4,836 parent or guardian in the household	Parent-perceived problem with drugs or alcohol by the adolescent	Violence exposure: sexual assault, physical assault, witnessed violence Mental health outcomes: PTSD, major depressive episode, SAD
Jester et al. (2000)	340 mother–child dyads	340 African American biological mothers	Self-report alcohol: Timeline FollowBack Method, MAST; frequency of other drug use	Family Environment Scale, intellectual stimulation and emotional support; Conflict Tactics Scale
McGlade et al. (2009)	119 infants of substance-using mothers, 238 matched controls	357 birth mothers	Any maternal disclosure of use or evidence of use among infant	Substantiated harm: physical abuse, neglect, sexual abuse, emotional abuse Foster care placement
McNichol & Tash (2001)	268 foster care children	Biological parents	Based on CPS records, caregivers grouped by prenatal exposure, active drug abuse, no drug use	CBCL, cognitive functioning/IQ, foster care outcomes: age and length of stay, gender differences
Ondersma (2002)	CPS neglect referred cases	203 female primary caregivers	Caregiver self-report based on lifetime abuse, problem in past 1–5 years, any treatment or self-help involvement	CPS codes for neglect; CWBS; Beavers family competence scale
Ondersma et al. (2006)	665 mother–child dyads	Biological mothers	MAST; child report (Things I Have Seen and Heard)	CBCL externalizing subscale; exposure to violence (Things I Have Seen and Heard TSH scale)
Ostler et al. (2007)	23 children, ages 7–14	15 biological mothers, 13 biological fathers, 2 mother's partners	Caregiver meth use documented in CPS file	Mental health functioning: CBCL; Children's Dissociative Checklist; TSCC
Scannapieco & Connell-Carrick (2007)	95 families, children ages 0–48 months	77 mothers, 8 fathers	Any caregiver drug use as noted in the CPS file	Substantiated vs. nonsubstantiated maltreatment based on caseworker report

Sprang et al. (2008)	1,127 children (average age = 5.1)	1,127 caregivers: biological, adoptive, and foster	Any caregiver drug use as noted in the CPS file	Trauma exposure: coding trauma events using Trauma Detail Form Trauma response: PTSD A1 and A2 response
Sun et al. (2001)	2,756 families	Caregivers of children referred to CPS	Based on CPS records, indication of alcohol abuse, drug abuse, both, or neither	Reason for referral to CPS: physical abuse, neglect, emotional abuse, sexual abuse, medical neglect
Van de Mark et al. (2005)	Children, ages 5–10	253 mothers in a larger research trial on mental health and violence	ASI Drug Composite	CBCL, BERS; lifetime exposure to physical or sexual abuse
Walsh et al. (2003)	9,953 households	Parents, mother, and father	Adults' retrospective accounts of parental substance use when they were growing up; self-reported "problem"	Adults' retrospective accounts of past child abuse or maltreatment, including physical abuse and sexual abuse
Wolock et al. (2001)	238 families	Any caregiver	Based on CPS records, any use, or self-reported at subsequent interviews	Based on CPS reports, abuse and neglect; rates of substantiated cases
Yampolskaya & Banks (2006)	3,646,450 children from birth to 18 in Florida	Documented caregiver in CPS case files	Based on CPS records, any drug or alcohol use by maltreatment perpetrator (in combination or alone)	Based on CPS records, type of maltreatment (abuse, neglect, threat), co-occurring maltreatment, recurrence of maltreatment, severity of type, severity of incident

Notes. CBCL = Child Behavior Checklist; IPV = intimate partner violence; NSCAW = National Survey of Child and Adolescent Well-Being; CIDI-SF = Composite International Diagnostic Interview Short Form; CPS = child protective services; *DSM–IV* = *Diagnostic and Statistical Manual of Mental Disorders* (4th ed.; American Psychiatric Association, 2000); CPR = Child Protection Register; PTSD = posttraumatic stress disorder; SAD = substance abuse disorder; MAST = Michigan Alcohol Screening Test; CWBS = Child Well-Being Scale; TSCC = Trauma Symptom Checklist for Children; ASI = Addiction Severity Index; BERS = Behavioral and Emotional Rating Scale.

Ondersma, Delaney-Black, Covington, Nordstrom, & Sokol, 2006; Ostler et al., 2007; Van de Mark et al., 2005). Other well-validated tools such as the Conflict Tactics Scale (Straus & Gelles, 1990) were used to examine exposure to specific violent acts between adult caregivers from which inferences of traumatic child witnessing could be made (Berger, 2005; Jester et al., 2000). In addition, other scales such as the Things I Have Seen and Heard Scale (Richters & Martinez, 1992) were used to assess exposure to violent activities among children, again allowing for inferences about child trauma or maltreatment (Connors-Burrow et al., 2009; Ondersma et al., 2006). However, the most consistent and widely used dependent variable was the investigator opinion about the presence of suspected or substantiated abuse and neglect charges. As earlier, the primary method of data collection for these variables was extraction from CPS records. This review also found more articles that focused on child welfare and safety issues than issues specific to psychosocial or behavioral outcomes such as trauma or specific developmental consequences.

Child Outcomes

As noted and shown in more detail in Table 2, much of the focus in the literature on the impact of caregiver substance misuse has focused on child maltreatment outcomes. For this analysis, the articles were organized by their outcome relative to child maltreatment, including (a) acts of maltreatment (physical abuse, sexual abuse, neglect, and frequency and severity of harm) or (b) psychosocial and behavioral outcomes (any and all emotional, cognitive, or behavioral response typically to either a maltreatment event or response to caregiver substance misuse).

Child maltreatment

Consistent with the search terms used for this review, the majority of the 23 articles (65%, $n = 15$) identified had dependent variables specific to child maltreatment. Caregiver substance misuse was strongly related to findings at the systems level with a number of studies focusing on the number of referrals and rereferrals to CPS for families with a substance-using caregiver compared to other families (Barth et al., 2006; McGlade, Ware, & Crawford, 2009; Yampolskaya & Banks, 2006). Consistently, having a substance-using caregiver was associated with a higher rate of referral to CPS, having a higher rate of rereferrals to CPS, and having a higher rate of substantiated cases within the system. With the estimated current lifetime average cost per victim of child maltreatment at more than $210,000 (Fang, Brown, Florence, & Mercy, 2012), it is imperative that child abuse prevention efforts begin to collaborate with treatment initiatives for substance-misusing caregivers as a way to enhance services to these at-risk families.

TABLE 2 Summary of Study Findings for Child Outcomes

Author	Prevalence of Substance Use	Primary Findings for Child Maltreatment	Primary Findings for Child Psychosocial or Behavioral Outcomes
Hanson et al. (2006)	18.4% overall for any family member (50.6% alcohol use, 19.1% drug use)	Parental substance use was significantly associated with a higher proportion of adolescents who reported sexual assault, physical assault, or witnessed violence.	Parental alcohol use—but not drug use—increased the likelihood of poor adolescent mental health outcomes, including PTSD, depression, and substance abuse disorders. Finally, those who both witnessed violence and had an alcohol using parent were most at risk for MDE.
Sprang et al. (2008)	68.1% substance use (not including alcohol)	Parental substance use was significantly associated with increased likelihood of physical abuse, child endangerment, witnessing domestic violence, chemical exposure, and exposure to multiple traumas.	Substance use by caregiver increased the likelihood of exposure to child traumatic events. Even though 52% of those in the non-substance-use group were exposed to a traumatic event, approximately half had documented responses that met PTSD Criterion A2, as opposed to almost two thirds of the substance-using caregiver group.
Jester et al. (2000)	13% heavy drinkers at 7-year follow-up; only 30% reported abstaining from any alcohol use	Frequent heavy alcohol use was highly correlated with increased witnessing of domestic violence.	Frequent heavy alcohol use was highly correlated with poor family functioning and decreased intellectual stimulation for children.
Ostler et al. (2007)	100% methamphetamine use	Not discussed	Findings indicated that more than half of this small sample of children scored in the clinically or borderline significant range on the CBCL and more than a third scored in the clinically or borderline significant range of the TSCC.

(*Continued*)

TABLE 2 (Continued)

Author	Prevalence of Substance Use	Primary Findings for Child Maltreatment	Primary Findings for Child Psychosocial or Behavioral Outcomes
McNichol & Tash (2001)	14% parental substance use	Not discussed	29.9% of foster care children scored in high range of CBCL compared to normative samples, and those with substance-using caregivers were more likely to be rated by teachers as having more behavioral and social problems.
Bailey et al. (2009)	Not provided	Not discussed	Parent substance use was related to increased child externalizing behavior (CBCL) in across-generation pairs. Grandparent substance use was related to parent externalizing behavior as adolescents, which was, in turn, related to their adult substance use. Parental adult substance use was associated with higher levels of adolescent externalizing behavior.
Van de Mark et al. (2005)	98% of parents treated for substance abuse problem	Not discussed	Higher maternal scores on ASI-Drug composite related to higher child resilient sores on CBCL and BERS. Eighty-six percent of children had scores in the average range on BERS.
McGlade et al. (2009)	100% self-reported mothers	A higher number of CPS referrals were made for infants of substance-using mothers (51%) compared to a matched control (6%) of non-substance-using mothers. After a number of adjustments for control variables, substance-using mothers were more likely to have substantiated claims of harm (highest for physical harm and neglect). A higher percentage of substance-using mothers lost custody of their infants to foster care (24%) during the follow-up, compared to control (2%) mothers.	Not discussed

Scannapieco & Connell-Carrick (2007)	100% families	Among substance-using caregivers, 52% had a substantiated maltreatment case with CPS. Study findings indicated that children of drug- and alcohol-using parents were more vulnerable, more fragile, and less protected. They also had less parenting capability, less resources, more parenting stress, and more stressful home environments. Parents who used drugs were also found to have more serious patterns of maltreatment and more chronic patterns of maltreatment based on the history of CPS reports.	Not discussed
Sun et al. (2001)	11% caregivers	Any type of caregiver alcohol or drug use was more likely to be associated with substantiated cases overall in CPS records, but particularly associated with physical abuse and neglect cases.	Not discussed
Connors-Burrow et al. (2009)	100% mothers	Recent substance abuse severity was associated with children's violence exposure, with exposure to violence being higher among children whose mothers reported having more days where they experienced problems related to their drug use. In addition, children's violence exposure was also greater among children whose mothers endorsed more beliefs associated with abusive and neglectful parenting on the AAPI-2.	Not discussed
Ondersma (2002)	31% substance abuse in family	Family substance abuse was a significant predictor of neglect, even higher when coupled with other negative life events.	Not discussed
Ondersma et al. (2006)	25.6% African American mothers MAST self-report, 48.6% child report	Maternal substance use variable explained nearly 30% of overall variance in child report of violence exposure; strongest predictors were witnessing drug deals and seeing drugs in the home.	Not discussed

(Continued)

TABLE 2 (Continued)

Author	Prevalence of Substance Use	Primary Findings for Child Maltreatment	Primary Findings for Child Psychosocial or Behavioral Outcomes
Crandall et al. (2006)	2% illicit drug use by mothers	Two risk factors were found to be significant in predicting injury requiring medical attention during the first year of life: (a) mother spanking child during the previous month and (b) alcohol use by mother during the previous month.	Not discussed
Walsh et al. (2003)	17.2% any substance use either parent	Parental substance abuse was strongly correlated with risk of exposure to both child physical and sexual abuse in a Canadian household survey.	Not discussed
Barth et al. (2006)	Not provided	Substance-using caregivers were more likely to have a report and a reoccurrence of child abuse or neglect with CPS, and the risks did not decrease among a sample who enrolled in substance abuse services.	Not discussed
Forrester (2000)	68% families	In a review of CPR records in a London district, substance-using families were significantly overrepresented in neglect cases (65.2%). Substance use was also present in all the cases of physical (100%) and the majority of emotional (66.7%) abuse cases.	Not discussed
DiLauro (2004)	21.4% any substance	Drug-using caregivers were more likely to neglect their children (78.3%) than the non-drug-using caregivers (46.8%), but they were less likely to cause physical harm abuse than the other group.	Not discussed

Yampolskaya & Banks (2006)	Not provided	In CPS records review of a large database, cases involving caregiver alcohol or drug use were associated with substantiated child neglect and threatened harm.	Not discussed
Berger (2005)	Not provided	Maternal alcohol abuse, not drug abuse and not paternal drug or alcohol abuse, was a strong predictor of increased physical abuse.	Not discussed
Wolock et al. (2001)	55% of families	Found that parental substance use is a unique contributor in a multivariate risk model to subsequent reports to CPS and to substantiation status, even when other factors associated with the family environment are controlled.	Not discussed
Gibbs et al. (2008)	13% of child maltreatment offenders	Offenders whose first child maltreatment experience involved substance use were more likely to have previously received a referral to substance abuse services. Levels of violence also varied, with those who committed both child and spouse abuse on the same day being more likely to have abused alcohol or drugs than those who only committed child maltreatment. Substance-using caregivers also were more likely to commit severe neglect and emotional abuse compared to non-substance-using caregivers.	Not discussed

Notes. PTSD = posttraumatic stress disorder; MDE = major depressive disorder; *DSM* = *Diagnostic and Statistical Manual of Mental Disorders*; CBCL = Child Behavior Checklist; TSCC = Trauma Symptom Checklist for Children; BERS = Behavioral and Emotional Rating Scale; CPS = child protective services; AAPI-2 = Adult-Adolescent Parenting Inventory-2; MAST = Michigan Alcohol Screening Test; CPR = Child Protection Register.

In addition to outcomes at the systems level, there are a number of important observations to make about consistent findings at the client level as well. Consistently, caregiver substance use was strongly and positively associated with an increased likelihood of children being exposed to violence, thus incurring risk of child trauma outcomes as well (Connors-Burrow et al., 2009; Hanson et al., 2006; Jester et al., 2000; Ondersma et al., 2006; Sprang, Staton-Tindall, & Clark, 2008). Some of these violent acts were associated with increased activities around the drug-using lifestyle as noted by Connors-Burrow et al. (2009), who used the Things I Have Seen and Heard Scale with robust predictors being events like witnessing types of drug deals go down in the home and seeing drugs in the home. Other violent acts were noted as domestic violence (Sprang et al., 2008), marital conflict or spouse abuse (Gibbs et al., 2008), and these events suggest a very different at-risk situation for children.

In addition to increased violence exposure, types of child maltreatment were also consistently identified among substance-misusing caregivers in these articles. Physical abuse and neglect were the most commonly reported types of child maltreatment associated with caregiver substance misuse in the articles reviewed for this analysis. The most prevalent form of study design for the reviewed articles was a secondary data analysis from CPS records, but the findings were consistent in showing association between increased child risk for physical abuse or neglect if there was at least one caregiver with substance misuse. Few of these studies, however, examined the other relevant family risk variables in expanded regression models to understand the unique contribution of the caregiver substance misuse. One exception is Wolock, Sherman, Feldman, and Metzger (2001), who found that substance use remains a significant and unique contributor to variance in substantiation risk even when other family risk variables are controlled. In addition, other studies have found that not only is the presence of alcohol or drug use in the home a major risk factor, but intensity and frequency of use can be associated with severity of maltreatment (Gibbs et al., 2008). However, given the wealth of other research findings about co-occurring risk factors in homes where caregivers are active substance misusers, the number of studies examining specific substance misuse effects was astonishingly low.

Psychosocial and Behavioral Child Outcomes

Although the primary search term used in this analysis was *child maltreatment*, a number of articles met inclusion criteria for the study that did not focus on the presence or nature of child maltreatment. These articles investigated the emotional, behavioral, or psychosocial response to either a maltreatment experience or the child's experience of living with a substance-using caregiver. In general, caregiver substance use had a negative impact on child's outcomes, but there was little consistency in the measurement of symptoms with the exception of the CBCL's internalizing and externalizing symptoms. Caregiver substance use was consistently related to higher, and even clinically significant, scores on CBCL measures in this analysis. A number of the studies in this analysis (Bailey et al., 2009) focused specifically on externalizing behavior. Although the CBCL was the most commonly instrument used, a few other studies also examined mental health symptoms, including posttraumatic stress disorder (PTSD), depression, adolescent substance use disorders, and overall family functioning. Consistently, caregiver substance use had a negative and consistent relationship with these disorders among children, and in some cases there was a cumulative effect where children who experienced witnessing violence and living with a substance-using caregiver were at greatest risk for developing a major depressive disorder (Hanson et al., 2006).

Findings Related to Targeted Practice Areas

Table 3 summarizes implications for practice as noted in each of the articles focused on caregiver substance use and child maltreatment. Across journals, the most commonly noted area for targeting implications of study findings was to adult substance users—these implications were typically focused on enhancing assessment and treatment practices for women and families. In addition to enhancing substance abuse treatment programming, a number of articles also included a specific focus on the inclusion of effective parenting as a critical element of treatment (Bailey et al., 2009; Berger, 2005; Connors-Burrow et al., 2009; DiLauro, 2004). In addition, other studies talked about other important co-occurring enhancements to treatment including mental health programming (Barth et al., 2006) and victimization/PTSD content (Connors-Burrow et al., 2009). Not surprising with the number of articles that focused on child maltreatment outcomes, a large number of articles also focused on implications for child welfare professionals. These findings highlight the need to increase access to evidence-based interventions (Berger, 2005), increase collaboration with other systems such as the military, which has had extensive experience with substance-using caregivers who have been child maltreatment perpetrators (Gibbs et al., 2008), and gain a better understanding of substance use within the context of the other risk factors of the home environment (Scannapieco & Connell-Carrick, 2007).

These articles provided some recommendations for practice specific to assessment that pertained to mental health professionals. However, implications for practice specific to children's mental health were lacking. Few articles made the connection between children's exposure to violence, chaotic lifestyles, and at-risk situations often associated with drug use to potential mental health consequences such as PTSD for children. As shown in Table 3, implications for child mental health professionals are rare—despite the obvious potential impairments associated with children's

TABLE 3 Summary of Practice Implications

Author	Journal	Implications for Practice						
		Child Welfare Professionals	Child Mental Health Professionals	Caregiver Substance Use Professionals	Systems/ Policy	Systems Integration	Assessment	Prevention
Bailey et al. (2009)	*Developmental Psychology*			X				
Barth et al. (2006)	*Journal of Substance Abuse Treatment*			X		X		
Berger (2005)	*Child Abuse and Neglect*	X			X			
Connors-Burrow et al. (2009)	*Journal of Pediatric Nursing*						X	
Crandall et al. (2006)	*Journal of Surgical Research*			X				
DiLauro (2004)	*Child Welfare League of America*				X			
Forrester (2000)	*Child Abuse Review*	X					X	
Gibbs et al. (2008)	*Child Maltreatment*	X				X	X	
Hanson et al. (2006)	*Addictive Behaviors*		X	X				
Jester et al. (2000)	*Alcoholism: Clinical and Experimental Research*			X				X
McGlade et al. (2009)	*Pediatrics*	X		X				
McNichol & Tash (2001)	*Child Welfare League of America*		X	X				
Ondersma (2002)	*American Journal of Orthopsychiatry*			X	X			
Ondersma et al. (2006)	*Journal of Traumatic Stress*		X	X		X		X
Ostler et al. (2007)	*Journal of the American Academy of Child & Adolescent Psychiatry*	X	X				X	
Scannapieco & Connell-Carrick (2007)	*Substance Use and Misuse*	X		X			X	
Sprang et al. (2008)	*Journal of Traumatic Stress*		X	X			X	
Sun et al. (2001)	*Child Welfare League of America*	X		X		X	X	
Van de Mark (2005)	*Journal of Community Psychology*			X			X	
Walsh et al. (2003)	*Child Abuse and Neglect*			X				
Wolock et al. (2001)	*Children and Youth Services Review*				X	X		
Yampolskaya & Banks (2006)	*Assessment*	X						X

experiences. In addition, few articles speak to the need to integrate resources across child welfare, children's mental health, and adult treatment services to enhance services for these at-risk families.

DISCUSSION

Although a number of literature reviews and meta-analyses have investigated the relationship between caregiver substance use and child maltreatment using preexisting frameworks derived from the larger fields of addiction or child welfare, this review enhances our understanding of these phenomenon by exploring the state of knowledge regarding the measurement of specific variables of interest, the range of child outcomes targeted for study, and how these studies might inform practice. To this end, this review highlights major challenges to researchers investigating the impact of caregiver substance misuse on child maltreatment in the area of measurement of key variables, and points to the need for more sophisticated, nuanced conceptual frameworks to understand the translational implications of the work.

Any understanding of the relationship between caregiver substance misuse and child maltreatment is advanced by efforts to improve the sensitivity and precision of measurement of key constructs. In the adult substance abuse treatment literature, dichotomous measures of substance use (any use: yes–no) have been supplanted by complex measures that lead to inferences about addiction severity. Research on neurodevelopment throughout childhood has likewise used complex measures of the behavioral outcomes of child maltreatment (Perry, 2009). However, when it comes to studies specifically examining combined caregiver substance misuse and child maltreatment, the reliance is on very weak and largely dichotomous measures. In addition, most of the findings are derived from unreliable secondary data sources that are dependent on "the presence of any substance use" in the file record. Although these studies make some contributions, our review strongly supports the claims made by Testa and Smith (2009) that the current state of measurement and assessment of substance use does very little to help us understand the mechanisms of action and risk for children within substance-using families unless used in concert with equally sophisticated child maltreatment and family environment measures. What makes this even more disturbing is that there are a wealth of sophisticated measures of adult substance misuse that can be readily employed in studying this problem. The reliance on child welfare data at this stage of the investigative process is equally disturbing. Entry of data by child welfare workers lacks validity or reliability as well as specificity. Thus, even sophisticated analysis of secondary data is likely working from poor data sources that will not allow exploration of complex associations, let alone cause–effect inferences.

We suggest that the future direction for examining the relationship between caregiver substance misuse must move beyond just conceptualizing substance use as an isolated factor. For example, many of the studies reviewed did not consider possible co-occurring conditions that could compromise the substance use and child maltreatment trajectories for these families. Substance use is likely to co-occur with high rates of poverty (Smyth, 1998) and other extreme living conditions, which might impact the life of children living in the home independent of the caregiver substance misuse (Sprang et al., 2008). Substance use is also likely to exist comorbidly with other mental conditions that can impact the caregiver's ability to successfully parent, such as depression, anxiety, and other disorders (Testa & Smith, 2009; Wells, 2009). Also, because some forms of substance use are illegal, it is likely to co-occur with high rates of criminal activity (CASA, 1998) and potentially high-risk behaviors in the home, which could create risk of harm for children living in the environment (Wells, 2009).

The majority of studies in the field have examined outcomes relative to acts of child maltreatment or the responsiveness of the child welfare system. Despite the inevitable consequences of those acts, very few articles illuminated the experiences of children living in the drug-using environment—referred to as "the elephant in the living room" by Kroll (2004). Only one third of the identified articles examined the other types of outcome such as mental health consequences of caregiver substance use for children or behavioral or emotional responsiveness. These studies used a wide range of standardized measures of child distress, but approached children in the sample as a homogenous target population. That is, differential findings by developmental stage were largely nonexistent, providing little direction for practitioners who work with children. These findings highlight the limitations of knowledge in this area, and explain the paucity of empirically validated practice standards for this population.

It is notable that we found that the majority of reviewed papers focused their attention on adult problems, such as the assessment and treatment of caregivers, and that so few considered the implications of substance misuse on the children in their samples. Adult caregivers certainly merited the attention of researchers and practitioners, but so did the children, especially because the putative goal of most studies was to understand the relationships of substance misuse to violence, child maltreatment, or both. Because the phenomenology of addiction-related maltreatment points to children as the "target," their systematic exclusion from these investigations and implications is striking and puzzling.

One possible explanation is that such exclusions are the product of "silo" effects that flow from the formal organization of research and practice domains. Often discipline driven, these orientations, in turn, affect researchers' fields of observation, the selected problems for investigation, and even the "samples" and "data" available for research studies. Indeed, real differences in training and orientations exist among those affiliated with the child welfare, child mental health, family studies, intimate partner violence, and addiction treatment sectors. Each field or subfield holds a long tradition of distinct research and practice emphases, which in turn, can direct the focus of theoretical and empirical attention (e.g., child–adult, males–females, individual–family, addict–enabler). Although there has been some progress toward seeing the broader systemic and ecological realities facing clients, arguably, many professionals continue to be directed into lesser and greater emphases that have more to do with their educational and training roots, than with real-world configurations—which, as shown by these findings, could limit the translational science of important cross-disciplinary work.

Even when the emphasis is primarily on children, the silo problem persists. Social work education, for example, has often bifurcated training between child mental health (for those pursuing clinical social work in community mental health) and child welfare training (for those heading for child protection, foster care, and adoption agencies), which might contribute to the divergence we see in the research findings presented here with researchers focusing on primarily one or the other in terms of dependent measures. The profession, in effect, has frequently advanced the idea that a distinct set of skills are necessary, to the point that the "child" population served by the profession requires two very different knowledge bases and skill sets, depending into which system the child presents.

Similarly, many community agencies are oriented to primarily serve either children or adults, and historically recruit professionals with those areas of distinct specialty training. Many financing mechanisms continue to consider the child as the "target" of care, and the caregiver as a "collateral," rather than the reality that both child and caregiver are targets needing intensive interventions, or that the "family" should be considered the target for change, and services reimbursed in ways that recognize this need. These differences go beyond just professional training. As mentioned earlier, the policy differences between child protection and family reunification play out throughout the practice and research environments. Researchers and practitioners "take sides" and fail to grasp the important interactional dimensions of caregiver–child problems and solutions. Instead, this review suggests that siloing continues to diminish the advance of science and practice.

Next Steps: Emphasis on the Role of Trauma

Although the search term *child trauma* did not yield a workable number of articles to be included in the final search for this article, four articles meeting study criteria under the *child maltreatment* search terms included PTSD, trauma exposure, or subthreshold traumatic stress symptoms as study variables. A trauma framework, however, might have significant conceptual, empirical, and translational utility for consideration for future research in this important area of study. Over the years, a number of studies have demonstrated a biopsychosocial interaction between traumatic stress and substance use, describing the relationship between the two conditions as reciprocal and complex (Grella, Stein, & Greenwell, 2005; Janikowski & Glover, 1994; Sprang et al., 2008). Studies have documented trauma exposure ranging from 30% to 90% in substance-using, treatment-seeking samples (Moncrieff, Drummond, Candy, Checinski, & Farmer, 1996; Najavits, Weiss, Shaw, & Muenz, 1998; Rice et al., 2001). The associations of caregiver substance misuse with trauma and other mental health problems are particularly prevalent among victimized women—a large number of whom are in the child welfare system (Logan, Walker, Jordan, & Leukefeld, 2006). Additionally, substance misuse could increase vulnerability to trauma exposure (beyond physical and sexual abuse) in adults who engage in unsafe and disinhibited behaviors while under the influence (Logan et al., 2006; Parks & Miller, 1997; Sprang et al., 2008), and in children, who are living with impaired caregivers who have high levels of parenting stress, poor impulse control, and who are inattentive to their needs (Sprang et al., 2008; Sprang et al., in press).

What is surprising from this review is the comparative absence of child trauma measures among the constellation of findings from studies of caregiver substance misuse and child maltreatment. The silo effect evident in this review is difficult to explain given the vast amount of attention that has been given to associations of child maltreatment with trauma conditions. Clearly, the advancement of meaningful translational research on this complex problem will require examination of caregiver substance misuse and related disorders, child maltreatment, and child mental health outcomes. Conveying useful information to practice or policy will depend on far more sophisticated research designs and methods in recognition of the advances in child development studies. Anchoring research and practice implications regarding caregiver substance misuse in a trauma framework provides an opportunity to direct assessment and treatment practices in an integrated way for the adult caregiver, the child, and the family in a manner that respects the physiological and psychological assault imposed by trauma exposure, and the intertwined challenges associated with recovery and treatment. In considering directions for future research and practice, for the trauma framework to add substantively to this field of work, two parallel missions must be achieved: (a) creation of a trauma-informed system of substance abuse care and (b) the development of evidence-based trauma treatment to treat comorbid traumatic stress and substance use disorders.

First, creating a system of care that is trauma informed mandates that services are grounded in the knowledge base of trauma, and consider the epidemiology, impact, relationship dynamics, and recovery process associated with trauma recovery. The development and maintenance of caregiver substance use disorders might represent maladaptive attempts to self-regulate affect and reexperiencing past traumatic events (Finklestein et al., 2004).

Trauma-informed systems place a priority on client safety, empowerment, and control, recognizing the loss of autonomy and self-efficacy induced by victimization. This type of approach for the family would focus on healing for the caregiver in an integrated model such as Seeking Safety (Najavits et al., 1998), as well as child or relationally focused treatments such as trauma focused-cognitive behavioral therapy (Cohen, Berliner, & Mannarino, 2010), Alternatives for Families, A Cognitive-Behavioral Therapy (AF–CBT; Kolko & Swenson, 2002), and child–parent psychotherapy (Lieberman & Van Horn, 2008).

Second, a trauma-informed system should provide evidence-based, trauma-specific services to address co-occurring traumatic stress conditions such as PTSD, acute stress disorder, and a range of substance use disorders. Although the fields of traumatic stress and substance misuse represent silos of knowledge regarding the etiology, assessment, and treatment of these conditions, the proposed approach requires integration of a family-focused trauma framework to reach caregiving parents and their children who are in need of trauma-focused services. As Finklestein et al. (2004) noted, "Both parallel and sequential approaches underestimate the realities of the close and often mutually reinforcing relationships between trauma and substance use" (p. 4). Thus, the synchronized delivery of services in an integrated model represents an opportunity to improve psychosocial and behavioral outcomes for caregivers and children.

Limitations

There are limits to any systematic literature search that could have impacted this review. Although considerable care was taken to identify and include all published peer-reviewed articles that would address the specified objectives of the review, it is possible that inaccurate or incomplete key wording in the editorial process could have prevented relevant studies from being detected. It is also conceivable that researchers from diverse disciplines utilize different nomenclatures to operationalize key concepts. This could have resulted in the omission of studies that could have shed some light on the impact of caregiver substance misuse on child outcomes from a unique perspective.

CONCLUSION

The current emphasis in the United States on translational science suggests that this important area of research focused on caregiver substance use and the impact on children must move beyond the simplistic measurement of both caregiver and child characteristics in cases of maltreatment. With agencies, practice providers, and researchers focused on either child maltreatment or on adult substance misuse patterns, there is a tendency to view study populations in disciplinary silos. What is needed for this version for translational, desiloized research to go forward is a focus on traumagenic conditions rather than on individuals who initiate and perpetuate the problem or on the individuals who suffer at the hands of those perpetrators. In many regards, the articles point to a disturbing lack of sophistication in the current state of the science in this area. Given the great wealth of findings in other research areas about the complexity of child outcomes from maltreatment and the complexity of adult substance misuse characteristics, this body of reviewed research is disappointing. The cost of future trauma of children and the dashed hopes for parental recovery demand a science that is commensurate with the scope of seriousness of the problems to be studied.

REFERENCES

Achenbach, T. (1991). *Manual for the Child Behavior Checklist/4–18 and 1991 profile*. Burlington, VT: University of Vermont, Department of Psychiatry.

American Psychiatric Association. (2000). *Diagnostic and statistical manual of mental disorders* (4th ed., text rev.). Washington, DC: Author.

Bailey, J. A., Hill, K. G., Oesterle, S., & Hawkins, J. D. (2009). Parenting practices and problem behavior across three generations: Monitoring, harsh discipline, and drug use in the intergenerational transmission of externalizing behavior. *Developmental Psychology, 45*(5), 1214–1226.

Barth, R. P., Gibbons, C., & Guo, S. (2006). Substance abuse treatment and the recurrence of maltreatment among caregivers with children living at home: A propensity score analysis. *Journal of Substance Abuse Treatment, 30*, 93–104.

Berger, L. M. (2005). Income, family characteristics, and physical violence toward children. *Child Abuse and Neglect, 29*, 107–133.

Cohen, J. A., Berliner, L., & Mannarino, A. (2010). Trauma focused CBT for children with co-occurring trauma and behavior problems. *Child Abuse & Neglect, 34*, 215–224.

Connors-Burrow, N. A., Johnson, B., & Whiteside-Mansell, L. (2009). Maternal substance abuse and children's exposure to violence. *Journal of Pediatric Nursing, 24*(5), 360–369.

Crandall, M., Chiu, B., & Sheehan, K. (2006). Injury in the first year of life: Risk factors and solutions for high-risk families. *Journal of Surgical Research, 133*, 7–10.

Department of Health and Human Services. (2009). *Protecting children in families affected by substance use disorders*. Washington, DC: Administration for Children and Families. Retrieved from http://www.childwelfare.gov/pubs/usermanuals/substanceuse/

DiLauro, M. (2004). Psychosocial factors associated with types of child maltreatment. *Child Welfare League of America, 83*(1), 69–99.

Dunn, S. R., Anda, R. F., Felitti, V. J., Croft, J. B., Edwards, V. J., & Giles, W. H. (2002). Growing up with parental alcohol abuse: Exposure to childhood abuse, neglect, and household dysfunction. *Child Abuse & Neglect, 25*, 1627–1640.

Fang, X., Brown, D. S., Florence, C. S., & Mercy, J. A. (2012). The economic burden of child maltreatment in the United States and implications for prevention. *Child Abuse and Neglect, 36*(2), 156–165. doi:10.1016/j.chiabu.1011.10.1006

Finklestein, N., Vandemark, N., Fallot, R., Brown, V., Cadiz, S., & Heckman, J. (2004). *Enhancing substance abuse treatment through integrated trauma treatment* (Rep. No. 270-2003-00001-0001). Rockville, MD: National Trauma Consortium for the Center for Substance Abuse Treatment.

Forrester, D. (2000). Parental substance misuse and child protection in a British sample. *Child Abuse Review, 9*, 235–246.

Gibbs, D. A., Martin, S. L., Johnson, R. E., Rentz, D., Clinton-Sherrod, M., & Hardison, J. (2008). Child maltreatment and substance abuse among US army soldiers. *Child Maltreatment, 13*(3), 259–268.

Grella, C. E., Stein, J. A., & Greenwell, L. (2005). Associations among childhood trauma, adolescent problem behaviors, and adverse adult outcomes in substance-abusing women offenders. *Psychology of Addictive Behaviors, 19*(1), 43–53.

Hanson, R. F., Self-Brown, S., Fricker-Elhai, A., Kilpatrick, D. G., Saunders, B. E., & Resnick, H. (2006). Relations among parental substance use, violence exposure, and mental health: The national survey of adolescents. *Addictive Behaviors, 31*, 1988–2001.

Huebner, B. M., & Gustafson, R. (2007). The effect of maternal incarceration on adult offspring involvement in the criminal justice system. *Journal of Criminal Justice, 35*, 283–296.

Janikowski, T. P., & Glover, N. M. (1994). Incest and substance abuse: Implications for treatment professionals. *Journal of Substance Abuse Treatment, 11*, 177–183.

Jester, J. M., Jacobson, S. W., Sokol, R. J., Tuttle, B. S., & Jacobson, J. L. (2000). The influence of maternal drinking and drug use on the quality of the home environment of school-aged children. *Alcoholism: Clinical and Experimental Research, 24*, 1187–1197.

Johnson, J. L., & Leff, M. L. (1999). Children of substance abusers: Overview of research findings. *Pediatrics, 103*, 1085–1099.

Kilpatrick, D., Acierno, R., Saunders, B., Resnick, H., & Best, C. (2000). Risk factors for adolescent substance abuse and dependence: Data from a national sample. *Journal of Consulting and Clinical Psychology, 68*(1), 19–30.

Kolko, D. J., & Swenson, C. C. (2002). *Assessing and treating physically abused children and their families: A cognitive behavioral approach*. Thousand Oaks, CA: Sage.

Kroll, B. (2004). Living with an elephant: Growing up with parental substance misuse. *Child and Family Social Work, 9*, 129–140.

Lieberman, A. F., & Van Horn, P. (2008). *Psychotherapy with infants and young children: Repairing the effects of stress and trauma on early attachment*. New York, NY: The Guilford Press.

Logan, T., Walker, R., Jordan, C., & Leukefeld, C. (2006). *Women and victimization: Contributing factors, interventions, and implications*. Washington, DC: American Psychological Association.

Magura, S., & Laudet, A. B. (1996). Parental substance abuse and child maltreatment: Review and implications for intervention. *Children and Youth Services Review, 18*, 193–220.

McGlade, A., Ware, R., & Crawford, M. (2009). Child protection outcomes for infants of substance-using mothers: A matched-cohort study. *Pediatrics, 124*, 285–293.

McNichol, T., & Tash, C. (2001). Parental substance abuse and the development of children in family foster care. *Child Welfare League of America, 80*(2), 239–256.

Moncrieff, J. D., Drummond, D. C., Candy, B., Checinski, K., & Farmer, R. (1996). Sexual abuse in people with alcohol problems: A study of prevalence of sexual abuse and its relationship to drinking behavior. *British Journal of Psychiatry, 169*, 355–360.

Murray, J., Janson, C., & Farrington, D. P. (2007). Crime in adult offspring of prisoners: A cross-national comparison of two longitudinal samples. *Criminal Justice and Behavior, 34*, 133–149.

Najavits, L. M., Weiss, R. D., Shaw, S. R., & Muenz, L. R. (1998). "Seeking safety": Outcome of a new cognitive-behavioral psychotherapy for women with posttraumatic stress disorder and substance dependence. *Journal of Traumatic Stress, 11*, 437–456.

National Center on Addiction and Substance Abuse. (1998). *Behind bars: Substance abuse and America's prison population* [Online]. Retrieved from http://www.casacolumbia.org/pdshopprov/files/5745.pdf

National Center on Addiction and Substance Abuse. (2005). *Family matters: Substance abuse and the American family* (CASA White Paper). New York, NY: Columbia University. Retrieved from http://www.casacolumbia.org/Absolutenm/articlefiles/380-family_matters_report.pdf

National Survey on Drug Use and Health. (2009). *Children living with substance-dependent or substance-abusing parents: 2002 to 2007* (National Survey on Drug Use and Health Report). Retrieved from http://www.samhsa.gov/data/2k9/SAparents/SAparents.htm

Ondersma, S. J. (2002). Predictors of neglect within low SES families: The importance of substance abuse. *American Journal of Orthopsychiatry, 72*(3), 383–391.

Ondersma, S. J., Delaney-Black, V., Covington, C. Y., Nordstrom, B., & Sokol, R. J. (2006). The association between caregiver substance abuse and self-reported violence exposure among young urban children. *Journal of Traumatic Stress, 19*(1), 107–118.

Ostler, T., Haight, W., Black, J., Choi, G., Kingery, L., & Sheridan, K. (2007). Case series: Mental health needs and perspectives of rural children reared by parents who abuse methamphetamine. *Journal of the Academy of Child and Adolescent Psychiatry, 46*(4), 500–507.

Parks, K. A., & Miller, B. A. (1997). Bar victimization of women. *Psychology of Women Quarterly, 21*, 509–525.

Perry, B. D. (2009). Examining child maltreatment through a neurodevelopmental lens: Clinical applications of the neurosequential model of therapeutics. *Journal of Loss and Trauma, 14*(4), 240–255.

Rice, C., Mohr, C. D., Del Boca, F. K., Mattson, M. E., Young, L., Brady, K. T., . . . Nickless, C. (2001). Self-reports of physical, sexual and emotional abuse in alcoholism treatment sample. *Journal of Studies on Alcohol, 61*, 114–123.

Richters, J. E., & Martinez, P. (1992). *Things I have seen and heard: A structured interview for assessing young children's violence exposure*. Rockville, MD: National Institute of Mental Health.

Scannapieco, M., & Connell-Carrick, K. (2007). Assessment of families who have substance abuse issues: Those who maltreat their infants and toddlers and those who do not. *Substance Use and Misuse, 42*, 1545–1553.

Smyth, N. (1998). Exploring the nature of the relationship between poverty and substance abuse: Knowns and unknowns. *Journal of Human Behavior in the Social Environment, 1*(1), 67–82.

Sprang, G., Clark, J., & Bass, S. (2005). Predicting the severity of child maltreatment using multidimensional assessment and measurement approaches. *Child Abuse and Neglect: An International Journal, 29*, 335–350.

Sprang, G., Staton-Tindall, M., & Clark, J. (2008). Trauma exposure and the drug endangered child. *Journal of Traumatic Stress, 21*, 1–7.

Sprang, G., Staton-Tindall, M., Gustman, B., Freer, B., Clark, J., Dye, H., & Sprang, K. (in press). The impact of trauma exposure on parenting stress in rural America. *Journal of Child and Adolescent Trauma.*

Straus, M. A., & Gelles, R. J. (1990). *Physical violence in American families: Risk factors and adaptation to violence in 8,145 families.* New Brunswick, NJ: Transaction.

Sun, A., Shillington, A. M., Hohman, M., & Jones, L. (2001). Caregiver AOD use, case substantiation, and AOD treatment: Studies based on two southwestern counties. *Child Welfare League of America, 80*(2), 151–177.

Testa, M. F., & Smith, B. (2009). Prevention and drug treatment. *The Future of Children, 19*(2), 147–167.

Van de Mark, N. R., Russell, L. A., O'Keefe, M., Finkelstein, N., Noether, C. D., & Gampel, J. C. (2005). Children of mothers with histories of substance abuse, mental illness, and trauma. *Journal of Community Psychology, 33*(4), 445–459.

Walsh, C., MacMillan, H. L., & Jamieson, E. (2003). The relationship between parental substance use and child maltreatment: Findings from the Ontario Health Supplement. *Child Abuse and Neglect, 27*, 1409–1425.

Wells, K. (2009). Substance abuse and child maltreatment. *Pediatric Clinics of North America, 56*, 345–362.

Widom, C. S., White, H. R., Czaja, S. J., & Marmorstein, N. R. (2007). Long-term effects of child abuse and neglect on alcohol use and excessive drinking in middle adulthood. *Journal of Studies on Alcohol and Drugs, 68*(3), 317–326.

Wolock, I., Sherman, P., Feldman, L. H., & Metzger, B. (2001). Child abuse and neglect referral patterns: A longitudinal study. *Children and Youth Services Review, 23*(1), 21–47.

Yampolskaya, S., & Banks, S. M. (2006). An assessment of the extent of child maltreatment using administrative databases. *Assessment, 13*(3), 342–355.

Family Structure, Substance Use, and Child Protective Services Involvement: Exploring Child Outcomes and Services

NATASHA MENDOZA, MSW, PhD
Assistant Professor of Social Work, College of Public Programs, Arizona State University, Phoenix, Arizona, USA

Using data from the National Survey on Child and Adolescent Well-Being (N = 5,501), this study explored caregiver substance use, family structure, and child well-being. Findings demonstrated that children of single mothers who use substances had higher externalized behavior problems than children of mothers with secondary caregivers in the home and who did not use substances. Children demonstrated more positive behavior and social skills in families without substance use. Single mothers with substance use accessed the most mental and behavioral health services and child welfare casework services compared to mothers who had available secondary caregivers and who did not use substances. Overall, this study demonstrated links among family structure, substance use, and child protective services involvement.

This document includes data from the National Survey on Child and Adolescent Well-Being that was developed under contract with the Administration on Children, Youth, and Families, U.S. Department of Health and Human Services (ACYF/DHHS). The data have been provided by the National Data Archive on Child Abuse and Neglect. The information and opinions expressed in the article reflect solely the position of the author. Nothing herein should be construed to indicate the support or endorsement of its content by ACYF/DHHS.

In 2010, 3.6 million children were subjects of at least one report to child protective services (CPS; U.S. Department of Health and Human Services [DHHS], Administration on Children, Youth and Families, Children's Bureau, 2011). Among the substantiated cases of child maltreatment reported each year in the United States, an estimated 81% of child maltreatment is the result of a parent's actions; commonly, a child's mother is identified as being the source (37%) of the abuse or neglect (DHHS, Administration on Children, Youth and Families, Children's Bureau, 2011). Mental and behavioral health issues, such as parental substance misuse or abuse, compound the problem, as these issues are clearly linked to the maltreatment of children (Child Welfare League of America, 2001; DHHS, 1999, 2005; DHHS, Administration on Children, Youth and Families, Children's Bureau, 2011). The 8 million children whose parents abuse substances (Substance Abuse and Mental Health Services Administration [SAMHSA], 2009) are more likely to face a variety of problems, including poor physical, intellectual, social, and emotional development, than are children living in families where substance use is not identified as problematic (DHHS Administration on Children, Youth and Families, Children's Bureau, 2009). Moreover, children involved with the child welfare system who have chemically dependent parents are more likely to be placed in foster care and remain there longer (DHHS, 1999). The Child Welfare League of America (2001) estimated that substance abuse exists in 40% to 80% of families that have substantiated cases of child maltreatment. Among single mothers who have limited support systems, problems of substance use and involvement in the child welfare system might add to an already complicated family situation. The purpose of this article was to begin exploring the complex nature of single motherhood, substance use, and child well-being among families involved with CPS.

PARENTAL SUBSTANCE USE AND CPS INVOLVEMENT

Children who reside with parents who use and misuse addictive and illegal substances are at an increased risk of physical abuse and neglect (DHHS, 2009; U.S. General Accounting Office, 1994), and research has shown that up to 79% of families involved with child welfare services are headed by caregivers who meet criteria for substance abuse (Besinger, Garland, Litrownik, & Landsverk, 1999). Homes in which substance abuse is present have been described as chaotic, unpredictable, inconsistent, and emotional (Breshears, Yeh, & Young, 2004). In addition, children who are endangered by parental drug use are at heightened risk of experiencing traumatic life events (Sprang, Staton-Tindall, & Clark, 2008). In this regard, Sprang and colleagues found that CPS-involved children who were identified as drug endangered were 4.77 times more likely to have experienced a traumatic event, 1.5 times more likely to have experienced physical abuse, 3.2 times more likely to have experienced violence in the home, 1.4 times more likely to have been placed in dangerous situations, and 60 times more likely to have been exposed to hazardous chemicals used in the manufacture of drugs. Furthermore, the authors reported that the rate of trauma exposure among CPS-involved children of substance-abusing parents is just under 74%, which "meets or exceeds the exposure rates of children living in war-torn areas such as Rwanda" (Sprang et al., 2008, p. 337). Ultimately, research has shown that for adult caregivers with substance abuse problems, maintaining sobriety is particularly difficult while they are involved with the child welfare system (Gregoire & Schultz, 2001).

When mothers experience problems related to substance use, CPS-involved families fare worse than families without such problems. Sun, Shillington, Hohman, and Jones (2001) conducted two studies examining caregiver alcohol and other drug (AOD) use, case substantiation for child abuse and neglect, and AOD treatment. The first study examined the effect of AOD use on CPS case substantiation among 2,756 families. Sun and colleagues wanted to determine if cases with indicated AOD use were more likely to be substantiated than cases that were not substantiated. They found that the odds of a case being substantiated as physical abuse or neglect were 96% higher when AOD use was indicated than when it was not. This suggests a strong link between AOD use and substantiated child abuse and neglect. The second study, with a sample consisting of 1,008 caregiving women, compared women in substance abuse treatment with CPS involvement to those not involved with CPS. They found that women in the CPS-involved group were significantly younger, had a higher mean number of children, were less likely to be employed, and were 1.5 times more likely to be referred to additional services post-AOD treatment. Women who reported being mandated to treatment were 2.5 times more likely to experience involvement with CPS. As discussed in the next section, single women in particular are faced with multiple challenges when substance use is problematic.

ABSENCE OF SECONDARY CAREGIVERS

For alcohol- and drug-involved families the lack of secondary caregivers could lead to negative child well-being outcomes. Based on 2010 census data, there are nearly 10 million single mothers in the United States; consequently, 23% of children live with only their mother (U.S. Bureau of the Census, 2010). Research has demonstrated that single mothers who have never been married have greater odds of substance abuse than married women (Afifi, Cox, & Enns, 2006). Furthermore, children who reside with a single parent (most often a mother) are more likely to experience physical abuse than children who live in two-parent households (i.e., 120% greater risk of experiencing maltreatment; Goldman, Salus, Wolcott, & Kennedy, 2003)

Over the past 40 years, the number of households headed by single mothers has grown from 3.4 million to nearly 10 million (U.S. Bureau of the Census, 2010). This statistic is of particular concern because children of single mothers are at greater risk for adverse consequences such as maltreatment due to parents' limited social, emotional, and financial resources (McLanahan, 1995; Teitler, Reichman, & Nepomnyaschy, 2004). Furthermore, research has shown that single women are at increased risk for a variety of negative psychosocial outcomes, and these issues might interfere with effective parenting. In one study, Cairney, Boyle, Offord, and Racine (2003) examined the potential mediating and moderating effects of stress and social support related to single parenthood among other outcomes. Their research addressed associations between family structure and exposure to current and past life stressors. Their secondary data analysis of the National Population Health Survey was conducted with subsamples of single mothers (n = 725) and married mothers (n = 2,231). Results indicated that single mothers were also more likely to be poor, younger, and generally less educated. Moreover, single mothers reported higher levels of stress, childhood adversity, less perceived social support, less interpersonal contact, and lower levels of social involvement (Cairney et al., 2003).

This study was intended as a step toward a better understanding of the complex nature of single motherhood, substance use, and child well-being among families involved with CPS. This study was purely exploratory with no a priori hypotheses being tested. Three aims were pursued: The first aim evaluated the impact of family structure (i.e., single mothers vs. mothers with available secondary caregivers) and mother's substance use (i.e., present or absent) on child measures of behavior and social skills. The second aim evaluated changes in child behavior and social skills over time. The third aim evaluated the extent to which the families utilized child- and adult-level services.

METHOD

Procedures

The National Survey of Child and Adolescent Well-Being (NSCAW) was developed by the DHHS in response to the Personal Responsibility and Work Opportunity Reconciliation Act of 1996. The survey is the first of its kind to capture the unique experiences of family members within child welfare and other community service systems (National Data Archive on Child Abuse and Neglect [NDACAN], 2002). The longitudinal study "examines the interplay among the history and characteristics of children and families, their experiences with the child welfare system, other concurrent life experiences, and outcomes" (NDACAN, 2002, p. 1).

Researchers at the NDACAN (2002) defined the NSCAW sample as a two-stage stratified design. The first stage involved dividing the United States into nine strata; eight of the strata were defined by states with the largest child welfare caseloads. The ninth stratum was made up of the remaining 42 states and the District of Columbia. The second stage of the design process involved forming primary sampling units (PSUs) from within each of the nine strata that were defined as "geographic areas that encompass the population served by a single child protective services (CPS) agency" (p. 17). To increase the chance of selecting areas with higher caseloads, the PSUs were chosen with a probability-proportionate-to-size procedure. The target population for the NSCAW CPS sample included "all children in the U.S. who are subjects of child abuse or neglect investigations (or assessments) conducted by CPS" (NDACAN, 2002, p. 22). As a result, the NSCAW CPS study sample is made up of 5,501 children. This study utilized restricted release data for the CPS sample available from Waves 1 through 4 that captured data from the child and the caregiver representing follow-up information collected approximately 2 to 36 months after the initial investigation was closed. Baseline data were used to describe the sample. Data from Waves 2 and 3 were used to describe services and data from Wave 4 captured outcomes of interest in this study.

Participants

Four subgroups were drawn from the larger NSCAW CPS sample. Participants were categorized as either a single mother or as a secondary caregiver, and as either a person who uses substances or as a person who does not use substances. In all four categories, a self-reported biological mother was identified as a primary caregiver. This information was available as part of the NSCAW Current Caregiver Instrument (CCI). To be in the single mother category, the primary caregiver was the self-reported biological mother and there was no secondary caregiver in the home. Inclusion in the opposite category meant that there was an identified secondary caregiver in the home in addition to the mother. In this study, the secondary caregiver included any other adult in the home who had a role in the caretaking of the child (e.g., father, grandparent). Caregivers were asked explicitly if the secondary caregiver had a role in caretaking. In the NSCAW sample, there were 143 mothers with available secondary caregivers (SC) and with identified substance use problem (SU), 382 mothers with SC and no SU, 719 single mothers with SU, and 1,945 single mothers with no SU. The total number of observations was 3,189 out of 5,501 children in the CPS sample. The decreased sample was due to the fact that not all primary caregivers were biological mothers. Data were representative of the national population of CPS-involved families (NDACAN, 2002).

Measures

Substance use

Inclusion criteria for substance use status were determined via the alcohol and drug dependence assessments that were part of the CCI Audio-Computer Assisted Self-Interview. A respondent was categorized as using substances if she answered "yes" to at least 1 of 24 different substance use problem instances over the past 12 months. For a respondent to be categorized as nonusing, she must have answered "no" to all 24 items (1 = yes, if any; 0 = no to all). For example, the individual might have indicated that she had been under the influence of alcohol or drugs in a situation where she could have been physically injured. Specific example items included the following:

- In the past 12 months, was there a time when your drinking [or drug use] or being hung over interfered with your work at school, or a job, or at home?
- During the past 12 months, was there a time when you were under the influence of alcohol [or drugs] in a situation where you could get hurt—like when driving a car or boat, using knives or guns or machinery, or anything else?
- During the past 12 months, did you have any emotional or psychological problems from using alcohol [or drugs], such as feeling uninterested in things, feeling depressed, suspicious of people, paranoid, or having strange ideas?

In this study, the instance of substance use occurred if the problematic situation happened at least once over the past year. In other words, an individual was judged to use substances if, over the past year, her life had been negatively impacted by her alcohol or drug use at least one time. It is important to note that the majority of people experiencing drug or alcohol-related problems experience them along a continuum of severity and might never meet an official diagnostic criterion.

Use of services

The instance of having received a specific service (e.g., one visit to a mental health provider) was measured via counts (1 = yes, reported service; 0 = no service). There were 64 service instances included in this analysis. Service instances were manually selected (i.e., the total number of "yes" responses to receiving a specific service in the past year or since the last interview) out of the NSCAW data set to first find appropriate survey items and then make a reasonable determination about the subcategory to which the service item belonged. There were three service subtypes for children and four service subtypes for adults (i.e., mental/behavioral health for adult and child, physical health of the child, child education, parent skill, concrete services, and casework). Service dose or amount received was not included as it varied across time or nature of service, or was missing. Categorizing services into subtypes was a subjective decision. Only dichotomous response survey items were included. For example, a visit to a physician for a physical examination would be categorized in the physical health subcategory. Examples of child mental and behavioral health subcategory items were "Child has been in a residential treatment center or group home," and "Child has been in a mental health center." The child education subcategory included items such as, "Child is currently receiving special education services or classes." Example of the adult mental or behavioral health subcategory services included items like, "Received treatment for a mental health problem." The adult casework subcategory included items such as, "Received parent aide services," and examples of concrete items were "Received food from community source" and "Received emergency shelter/housing." Following the development of subcategory counts, the services were tested to assess the presence of underlying latent factors. Factor loadings suggested the presence of two latent factors representing child and adult-specific services. These groupings were analyzed separately.

Child Behavior Checklist

The Child Behavior Checklist (CBCL) was designed to measure and define behavioral problems in children ages 2 to 18 (Achenbach, 1991). The instrument measured behavior over nine domains of social withdrawal, somatic complaints, anxious/depressed, social problems, thought problems, attention problems, delinquent behavior, aggressive behaviors, and other problems (Achenbach, 1991). The CBCL assessed perceptions of the parent, teacher, and child. In this study, the current caregiver's perceptions of child behavior were analyzed. Individual items and responses varied throughout the CBCL, examples of CBCL aggressive behavior items included "Child has temper tantrums," "Child hits others," and "Child is easily frustrated." Caregivers would then rate their child as manifesting these behaviors within the past 2 months as *often, sometimes,* or *never* (Love et al., 2002). Items on the measure were coded from 0 (*not true in the last 2 months*) to 2 (*very true or often true in the last 2 months*). For the NSCAW sample, internal consistency ranged from .80 to .96 over measurement domains (NDACAN, 2002). This study utilized T scores (T scores have $M = 50$ and $SD = 10$). For externalizing problems and internalizing problems, T scores less than 60 were considered in the normal range, 60 to 63 represented borderline scores, and scores greater than 63 were in the clinical range (Injury Prevention Research Center, 2009). Because children of different ages were administered different versions of the scales, all children's scores were entered into two analyzable variables that represented T scores for Internalizing and Externalizing scales.

Social Skills Rating System

The Social Skills Rating System (SSRS) measured children's social skills from different adult perspectives (Gresham & Elliott, 1990). Within NSCAW, caregivers and teachers addressed social skills, based on the child's social behavior, over domains of cooperation, assertion, responsibility, and self-control (Gresham & Elliott, 1990). The current caregiver's report was selected for analysis. Respondents reported on a 3-point scale (i.e., 0 = *never*, 1 = *sometimes*, 2 = *very often*). The SSRS consisted of three areas: social skills, behavior problems, and academic competence (Gresham & Elliott, 1990). Depending on the age of the child, the instrument included 38 to 40 items. Example items were "How often does the child appear self-confident in social interactions with opposite-sex friends?," "How often does the child receive criticism well?," and "How often does the child wait his or her turn in games or other activities?" The SSRS has been standardized with more than 5,000 individuals including children, parents, and caregivers, with a test–retest reliability of .87. The NSCAW sample demonstrated internal consistency of the measure at an alpha of .90 and .87 for preschoolers and secondary school-age children, respectively. This study utilized the standard scores based on the Social Skills and Problem Behavior subscales for each age group (i.e., 3–5, 6–10, 11+). All raw scores were converted into standard scores (M = 100, SD = 15). Standard scores could range from 40 to 130 with most children falling between 70 and 130 (95%). Scores below 85 were below average, scores between 85 and 115 were average, and scores above 115 reflected above-average behavior (Gresham & Elliott, 1990). This research assumed that a standard score attained by a 5-year-old was comparable to the same standard score attained by a 13-year-old. Thus, standard scores for all children were included in one variable for analysis. Responses such as "Don't know" or refusal responses were treated as missing.

Analytical Considerations

All analytical procedures were performed in consideration of complex sampling weights, strata, and PSUs. Normally, the most appropriate test for comparing multiple means across groups would be an analysis of variance (ANOVA). However, when an ANOVA is run the underlying assumption is that the data are independent and not correlated. With complex samples, this assumption is by default violated because of intraclass correlation.

As standard errors and *p* values would be biased if the data were run without consideration of the complex sample, the tests herein were regressions where the observed measures of the CBCL and the SSRS were regressed on group type. Statistics were also performed in which services were regressed on group type. In each case, the referent group was mothers with SC and no SU. Some data were missing due to stratum with limited or single sampling units. With respect to services, the study utilized negative binomial regression because the dependent variable was a nonnegative count variable (StataCorp, 2007). Analyzing count data with ordinary least squares regression would have been inappropriate for the service variable because the distribution was skewed. When the variance is larger than the mean, a negative binomial approach is preferred over a Poisson regression.

Missing Data Considerations

Perhaps one of the most considerable limitations of the NSCAW was missing data. On a given measured variable used, there were between 16.03% and 47.83% missing data. The missing data problem was compounded with group constraints (i.e., single mothers vs. mothers with SC and SU vs. no SU). Within groups, missing data were not just an issue at the child level; missing data became problematic where strata were no longer represented for a given variable of interest. To address issues with missing data, statistical tests were run using listwise deleted data.

RESULTS

Descriptive Statistics: Demographics

Demographic information was weighted. Summary statistics were output by STATA 10 in consideration of the complex sample strata, clusters, and case weights. This section presents a broad picture of the overall NSCAW CPS sample as well as notable demographic proportions for each group of interest in the study. Demographics included herein were based on the initial (Wave I) assessment.

Children's ages ranged from 1 to 15 and proportions of children at a given age ranged from 5.8% to 8.1%. Boys and girls were evenly represented in NSCAW at Wave 1. For listwise analyses, children younger than 3 were not included due to measurement constraints. However, descriptive statistics were reported for the entire CPS data set, thus the demographics represent the sample in its entirety.

In the full NSCAW CPS sample, all caregiver age groups were represented. However, in the study groups (see Table 1), the age group > 54 was not available as there were no individual cases of caregivers representing this age group in each of the four subcategories of interest. Out of the four group

TABLE 1 Caregiver Demographics

Demographics	Full NSCAW Sample[a] %	Single Mothers, No SU[b] %	Single Mothers With SU[c] %	Mothers With SC & SU[d] %	Mothers With SC, No SU[e] %
Age					
<35 years	58.39	65.54	63.96	81.23	73.55
35–44 years	28.25	29.53	31.59	16.98	21.62
45–54 years	9.05	4.91	4.44	1.77	4.82
>54 years	4.29	—	—	—	—
Percent race					
Native Indian/Alaskan	6.23	3.89	7.16	3.47	4.89
Asian/Hawaiian/Pacific Islander	2.40	2.30	0.46	0.64	5.08
Black	28.89	24.97	30.86	17.88	24.84
White	55.78	55.51	50.60	68.92	61.00
Other	6.68	13.31	10.89	9.06	4.17
Hispanic	18.22	18.93	12.52	17.27	8.28
Black	27.87	24.75	30.31	17.80	24.80
White	46.98	49.87	48.13	58.70	56.89
Other	6.91	6.44	9.01	6.21	10.01
Percent employment/education					
Employment category					
Full time	42.08	43.46	28.94	36.52	39.39
Part time	14.79	15.90	17.43	9.62	14.41
Do not work	29.43	26.18	37.25	26.18	25.75
Unemployed	10.60	11.95	11.35	26.72	15.85
Other	3.08	2.48	5.01	0.00	4.58
Current caregiver highest degree					
Ungraded place	0.13	0.00	0.00	—	—
Less than high school	29.07	30.84	35.23	37.62	31.61
High school	44.84	44.24	45.06	49.61	44.64
High school +	25.94	24.68	19.57	12.76	23.74

Notes. "Ungraded" examples include special education for students who are not mainstreamed, alternative schools aimed at helping high school-age adolescents meet minimal requirements for graduation or get a general equivalency diploma, and education services provided in residential treatment facilities. NSCAW = National Survey of Child and Adolescent Well-Being; SU = substance use; SC = secondary caregivers; — = no weighted proportions available.

[a]*N* = 5,501. [b]*N* = 1,945. [c]*N* = 719. [d]*N* = 143. [e]*N* = 382.

types, mothers with SC and SU were more likely to be among the youngest caregivers. Most caregivers involved with CPS were younger than 35.

Caregiver race variables showed that most people involved with CPS identified as White. The second largest group identified as Black followed by Hispanics. For all groups, the lowest proportion was of Asian/Hawaiian/Pacific Islanders.

In terms of employment, most caregivers were working full time. The next most prevalent category of work status was caregivers who did not work. Unemployment rates of all groups, except for mothers with SC who were using substances, were lower than "do not work" categories. Most primary caregivers in the NSCAW CPS sample had a high school education. Single mothers with no SU appeared to be the most educated out of the four study groups.

Descriptive Statistics: Child Welfare Data

Child welfare descriptive data included available information about placement type at initial assessment (Wave I) as well as percentage of child abuse and neglect substantiated by group type. However, there was limited information available about the type of initial placements by group. The most complete information came from the full NSCAW CPS sample. The reason for limited data was due to the inability to calculate weighted proportions when, in some strata, there were no cases represented. In the full NSCAW CPS sample, 88.20% of children were not in placement. Among the children in placement, 45.43% of children were placed in foster care followed by kinship care (38.16%; i.e., with a family member or close friend of the family of origin), group home (10.15%), and all other types of placement (6.24%). The only information available with respect to the four groups of interest was for mothers with SC and no SU. In this group, a large majority (93.19%) of children who were placed out of the home were in kinship care settings.

Reasons for CPS referral based on available data indicated that the majority of cases substantiated in the full NSCAW CPS sample at Wave I were either physical neglect or neglect with no supervision (22.87% and 27.82%, respectively). For single mothers with no SU, the majority of substantiated cases were for physical maltreatment (81.24%), followed by neglect (17.77%). Single mothers with SU demonstrated reports at 65.34% physical neglect and 34.65% neglect with no supervision cases. Perhaps the most interesting descriptive statistic was that 77.56% of the cases in homes of mothers with SC and no SU were substantiated for sexual abuse (followed by 20.81% substantiated for physical maltreatment).

Aim 1: Impact of Family Structure and Substance Use on Child Behavior and Social Skills

As shown in Table 2 the only significant finding for child behavior and social skills was that children in families headed by single mothers with SU demonstrated significantly higher externalized behavior at Wave I, compared to children in families headed by mothers with SC and no SU.

Aim 2: Changes in Child Behavior and Social Skills

In terms of change over time, paired sample *t* tests in Table 3 indicated that there was an overall decrease in externalized and internalized problem behaviors and an overall increase in social skills across the NSCAW sample

TABLE 2 Child Behavior Checklist and Social Skills Rating System by Group Type: Wave 1

Observed Measures Regressed on Group Type, Wave I	*b*	*SE*	*t*
Internalized CBCL Wave 1			
Single mothers, no SU[a]	−0.49	1.32	−0.37
Mothers with SC and SU[b]	2.05	2.48	0.82
Single mothers with SU[c]	2.33	1.36	1.71
Constant	54.09		
Externalized CBCL Wave I			
Single mothers, no SU	−1.49	1.20	−1.24
Mothers with SC and SU	1.94	2.27	0.86
Single mothers with SU	2.66	1.24	2.14*
Constant	57.50		
Social Skills Wave I			
Single mothers, no SU	0.10	1.72	0.06
Mothers with SC and SU	−0.43	3.01	−0.14
Single mothers with SU	−2.06	1.93	−1.06
Constant	91.06		

Notes. CBCL = Child Behavior Checklist; SU = substance use; SC = secondary caregiver.
[a]$n = 1{,}945$. [b]$n = 143$. [c]$n = 719$.
*$p \leq .05$, referent group = mothers with an available SC and no SU ($n = 382$).

as a whole from the initial (Wave I) assessment to the 36-month follow-up assessment (Wave IV). Paired sample *t*-test comparisons for the four subgroups for each outcome variable revealed four significant findings. First, for externalized problem behaviors, significant decreases over time were evident for both children of single mothers with no SU and those of single mothers with SU. For the internalized problem behaviors variable, there was a significant decrease only for the children of single mothers with no SU. Finally, for the social skills variable, there was a significant increase evident for only the children of mothers with SC and no SU.

Aim 3: Comparing Services Used

There were three service subtypes for children (i.e., mental or behavioral health, physical health, education) and four service subtypes for adults (i.e., mental or behavioral health, parent skill, concrete services, and casework). Services were analyzed as cumulative counts of service instances collapsed across 18 months after the close of the initial investigation. For all groups receiving child services, there were no significant differences in service instances when compared to mothers with SC and no SU (i.e., the referent group). With respect to adult services, three findings emerged (see Table 4). Single mothers with SU, the group with the highest level of presumed stressors, received on average significantly more casework services and adult mental and behavioral health services when compared to the referent group of mothers with SC and no SU. In addition, mothers with SC and with SU received more parent skill services, compared to mothers with SC and no SU.

TABLE 3 Family Structure and Substance Use Child Behavior Checklist Subscales and Social Skills Rating System: Waves I and IV

Family	CBCL Externalized Subscale Wave I	CBCL Externalized Subscale Wave IV	*t*	*df*
Single mothers, no SU[a]	56.27 (11.94)	54.68 (11.86)	2.30**	81
Single mothers with SU[b]	60.34 (11.37)	57.67 (10.66)	2.75*	80
Mothers with SC, no SU[c]	57.87 (11.98)	55.87 (10.39)	1.00	71
Mothers with SC and SU[d]	58.65 (—)	58.08 (—)	0.44	42
Complete NSCAW sample[e]	57.36 (12.05)	55.76 (11.74)	3.32**	83
	CBCL Internalized Subscale Wave I	CBCL Internalized Subscale Wave IV	*t*	*df*
Single mothers, no SU	53.66 (11.96)	51.39 (11.43)	4.21**	81
Single mothers with SU	56.27 (9.72)	54.64 (10.66)	1.60	80
Mothers with SC, no SU	54.50 (11.80)	52.59 (10.15)	1.82	71
Mothers with SC and SU	55.38 (—)	54.02 (—)	0.71	42
Complete NSCAW sample	54.26 (11.48)	52.19 (11.19)	5.49**	83
	Social Skills Wave I	Social Skills Wave IV	*t*	*df*
Single mothers, no SU	92.17 (14.19)	94.05 (15.61)	−1.59	70
Single mothers with SU	88.67 (14.50)	91.05 (14.27)	−1.69	79
Mothers with SC, no SU	90.38 (16.82)	94.08 (17.28)	−6.40**	81
Mothers with SC and SU	91.92 (—)	92.50 (—)	(—)	37
Complete NSCAW sample	90.15 (16.16)	93.20 (16.36)	−6.24**	83

Notes. CBCL = Child Behavior Checklist; SU = substance use; SC = secondary caregiver; NSCAW = National Survey of Child and Adolescent Well-Being; — = missing data because of stratum with single sampling unit. Standard deviations appear in parentheses below means. Degrees of freedom represent the number of primary sampling units minus the available strata.

[a] $n = 1,945$. [b] $n = 719$. [c] $n = 382$. [d] $n = 143$. [e] $N = 5,501$.

*$p \leq .01$. **$p \leq .001$.

DISCUSSION

This study addressed three specific aims. The first aim was to evaluate the impact of family structure and mother's substance use on measures of child behavior and social skills. Findings at the initial assessment period

TABLE 4 Adult Services Regressed on Group Type

Adult Service Regressed on Group Type (negative binomial regression)	*b*	*SE*	*t*
Parent skill			
Single mothers, no SU[a]	−0.20	0.14	−1.36
Mothers with SC and SU[b]	0.75	0.31	2.43**
Single mothers with SU[c]	0.36	0.21	1.66
Constant	−0.74		
Concrete service			
Single mothers, no SU	−0.11	0.14	−0.83
Mothers with SC and SU	0.24	0.20	1.19
Single mothers with SU	0.13	0.14	0.92
Constant	0.45		
Casework			
Single mothers, no SU	−0.20	0.16	−1.22
Mothers with SC and SU	0.38	0.30	1.26
Single mothers with SU	0.45	0.20	2.17*
Constant	−0.57		
Adult mental/behavioral health			
Single mothers, no SU	−0.06	0.20	−0.30
Mothers with SC and SU	0.73	0.41	1.77
Single mothers with SU	0.47	0.21	2.19*
Constant	−0.64		

Notes. Referent group = mothers with an SC and no SU ($n = 382$). SU = substance use; SC = secondary caregiver.
[a]$n = 1{,}945$. [b]$n = 143$. [c]$n = 719$.
*$p \leq .05$. **$p \leq .01$.

demonstrated that children with single mothers who used substances had higher externalized behavior than children with mothers with SC who did not use substances. This finding is in line with research suggesting a link between mother's substance abuse and increased risk for the child (McLanahan, 1995; Teitler et al., 2004). Future research in this domain should focus on building a clearer understanding of confounders (e.g., social capital, socioeconomic status, child gender) that might further impact child well-being.

The second aim of this study was to evaluate changes in child behavior and social skills over time. Children in this sample of CPS-involved families evidenced significant decreases in externalized and internalized behavior and increases in social skills over the assessment period (36 months). Looking specifically at the subgroup of single mothers with no SU, children showed significantly lowered external and internalized behavior problems over time. The children of single mothers with SU demonstrated significantly lowered externalized scores and the children of the mothers with SC and no SU showed significantly higher social skills over time. There might be several reasons for these outcomes. Children might simply mature out of problem behaviors and learn more social skills. It could also be the case that child welfare involvement and social services have some impact in helping children make gains as they mature. The impact of child welfare involvement on child behavior outcomes has demonstrated mixed results. A study conducted by Cheng and Lo (2010) utilizing data from the NSCAW examined the effect of child welfare services on adolescent behavior (i.e., alcohol use) and demonstrated no significant impact. Clearly, the impact of CPS or child welfare involvement on child behavior remains a question for future research.

The third aim of this study was to compare service use across groups of mothers. A noteworthy finding was that single mothers with SU were found to have more frequent use of both casework and mental or behavioral health services compared to mothers with SC and no SU. In addition, mothers with SC who used substances were using parent skills services at a greater frequency than the mothers with SC who did not use substances. Sun and colleagues (2001) demonstrated that women who were involved with CPS were 1.5 times more likely than women not involved with CPS to be referred to additional services post-AOD treatment. Women who reported being mandated to treatment were 2.5 times more likely to experience involvement with CPS. In each study, the group potentially most in need of services was indeed utilizing them. Ultimately, the impact of services in different family structures and with different levels of substance use are important issues to explore because they raise questions about service match and the need for services tailored to meet specific needs of the family.

Study Limitations

This was a secondary data analysis, which has obvious limitations as to the nature of collected data and data analysis. Statistical power might have been an issue with findings specific to the two smaller groups of women who had available secondary caregivers. Further, the presence of missing data could have introduced a level of bias in these results. Although attempts were made to address the missing data issue (i.e., listwise deletion), the reader should make note of this particular limitation, not only with the current effort but in all studies using NSCAW data. The way in which services were operationalized was another potential limitation. Service instances were manually selected from the large survey and then subjectively reduced into service categories such as mental or behavioral health. Said another way, subjective decisions were made about how services were categorized. Then, services were analyzed as counts within said categories. There was no way to compare "dosage" between differing service types. There was also a need for a more clearly articulated way to measure services across type and purpose.

Although this study provided some important initial analyses, there was also a potential for confounding variables that might have influenced the results, such as placement moves, characteristics of secondary caregivers (partners or spouses vs. grandparents or other adults), service referral, service dose, or child age and gender. Not accounting for type of substances used by the mothers might have introduced additional bias, as well as lack of measures addressing the perceived social support experienced by mothers.

CONCLUSION

This research was a descriptive and preliminary look at family structure and substance use related to child outcomes among families involved with CPS based on available information provided in a national data set. The results should be considered a starting place for future research that examines the role of social support with child outcomes for substance-using mothers who are involved with CPS. Continued research in areas examining social support and its impact on child outcomes with nationally representative samples is clearly needed, as is the need to examine the impact of different substances used by mothers involved in CPS. Haight, Carter-Black, and Sheridan (2009) qualitatively explored the experiences of mothers addicted to methamphetamines. The authors suggested that, for these women, engaging in services was an important goal. Many of the women endangered their children through their substance abuse because their ability to think rationally and use good judgment was often missing. However, their love and commitment to their children was evident. For the women, recovery was only possible with significant external social supports. Identifying mothers needing such support and offering appropriate support for them and their children is a critical next step.

REFERENCES

Achenbach, T. M. (1991). *Manual for the Child Behavior Checklist/4–18 and 1991 profile*. Burlington, VT: University of Vermont, Department of Psychiatry.

Afifi, T. O., Cox, B. J., & Enns, M. W. (2006). Mental health profiles among married, never-married, and separated/divorced mothers in a nationally representative sample. *Social Psychiatry & Psychiatric Epidemiology, 41*, 122–129.

Besinger, B. A., Garland, A. F., Litrownik, A. J., & Landsverk, J. A. (1999). Caregiver substance abuse among maltreated children placed in out-of-home care. *Child Welfare, 128*, 221–239.

Breshears, E. M., Yeh, S., & Young, N. K. (2004). *Understanding substance abuse and facilitating recovery: A guide for child welfare workers*. Rockville, MD: Substance Abuse and Mental Health Services Administration.

Cairney, J., Boyle, M., Offord, D. R., & Racine, Y. (2003). Stress, social support, and depression in single and married mothers. *Social Psychiatry and Psychiatric Epidemiology, 38*, 442–449.

Cheng, T. C., & Lo, C. C. (2010). The roles of parenting and child welfare services in alcohol use by adolescents. *Children and Youth Services Review, 32*, 32–43.

Child Welfare League of America. (2001). *Alcohol, other drugs, & child welfare.* Washington, DC: Author. Retrieved from http://www.cwla.org/programs/bhd/aodbrochure.pdf

Goldman, J., Salus, M. K., Wolcott, D., & Kennedy, K. Y. (2003). *A coordinated response to child abuse and neglect: The foundation for practice.* Washington, DC: U.S. Department of Health and Human Services, Administration for Children and Families.

Gregoire, K., & Schultz, D. J. (2001). Substance-abusing child welfare parents: Treatment and child placement outcomes. *Child Welfare, 80*, 433–452.

Gresham, F. M., & Elliott, S. N. (1990). *Social Skills Rating System manual.* Circle Pines, MN: American Guidance Service.

Haight, W. L., Carter-Black, J. D., & Sheridan, K. (2009). Mothers' experience of methamphetamine addiction: A case-based analysis of rural, midwestern women. *Children and Youth Services Review, 31*, 71.

Injury Prevention Research Center. (2009). *Description of measure: Child Behavior Checklist Achenbach, T.M., 1991.* Retrieved from http://www.iprc.unc.edu/longscan/

Love, J. M., Kisker, E. E., Ross, C. M., Schochet, P. Z., Brooks-Gunn, J., Paulsell, D., . . . Brady-Smith, C. (2002). *Making a difference in the lives of infants and toddlers and their families: Vol. II: Final technical report appendixes.* Washington, DC: Department of Health and Human Services, Administration for Children and Families; Office of Planning, Research and Evaluation; Child Outcomes Research and Evaluation; Administration on Children, Youth, and Families; Head Start Bureau.

McLanahan, S. (1995). The consequences of non marital childbearing for women, children, and society. In National Center for Health Statistics (Ed.), *Report to Congress on out-of-wedlock childbearing* (pp. 229–237). Hyattsville, MD: National Center for Health Statistics.

National Data Archive on Child Abuse and Neglect. (2002). *The National Survey of Child and Adolescent Well-Being (NSCAW) sampling frame data request specifications.* Ithaca, NY: Author.

Personal Responsibility and Work Opportunity Reconciliation Act of 1996, Pub. L. No. 104-193 (1996).

Sprang, G., Staton-Tindall, M., & Clark, J. (2008). Trauma exposure and the drug endangered child. *Journal of Traumatic Stress, 21*, 337.

StataCorp. (2007). *Stata statistical software: Release 10.* College Station, TX: StataCorp LP.

Substance Abuse and Mental Health Services Administration, Office of Applied Studies. (2009). *The NSDUH report: Children living with substance-dependent or substance-abusing parents: 2002 to 2007.* Rockville, MD: Author.

Sun, A. P., Shillington, A. M., Hohman, M., & Jones, L. (2001). Caregiver AOD use, case substantiation, and AOD treatment: Studies based on two southwestern counties. *Child Welfare, 80*, 151–177.

Teitler, J. O., Reichman, N. E., & Nepomnyaschy, L. (2004). Sources of support, child care, and hardship among unwed mothers, 1999–2000. *Social Service Review, 78*, 125–148.

U.S. Bureau of the Census. (2010). March 2010 current population survey: America's families and living arrangements: 2010, Table C9, Children by presence and type of parents, race, and Hispanic origin: 2010. Retrieved from http://www.census.gov/population/www/socdemo/hhfam/cps2010.html

U.S. Department of Health and Human Services. (1999). *Blending perspectives and building common ground. A report to Congress on substance abuse and child protection*. Washington, DC: U.S. Government Printing Office.

U.S. Department of Health and Human Services. (2005). *Child maltreatment*. Washington, DC: U.S. Government Printing Office. Retrieved from http://www.acf.hhs.gov/programs/cb/pubs/cm05/index.htm

U.S. Department of Health and Human Services, Administration on Children, Youth and Families, Children's Bureau. (2009). *Protecting children in families affected by substance use disorders*. Retrieved from http://www.childwelfare.gov/pubs/usermanuals/substanceuse/substanceuse.pdf

U.S. Department of Health and Human Services, Administration on Children, Youth and Families, Children's Bureau. (2011). *Child maltreatment 2010*. Retrieved from http://www.acf.hhs.gov/programs/cb/stats_research/index.htm#can

U.S. General Accounting Office. (1994). *Foster care: Parental drug abuse has alarming impact on young children* (GAO/HEHS Rep. No. 94-89). Washington, DC: Author.

Puerto Rican Parenting and Acculturation in Families Experiencing Substance Use and Intimate Partner Violence

CRISTINA MOGRO-WILSON, PhD, MSW
Assistant Professor, School of Social Work, University of Connecticut, West Hartford, Connecticut, USA

LIRIO K. NEGRONI, PhD, MSW
Associate Professor, School of Social Work, University of Connecticut, West Hartford, Connecticut, USA

MICHIE N. HESSELBROCK, PhD, MSW
Emeritus Professor, School of Social Work, University of Connecticut, West Hartford, Connecticut, USA

This study investigated Puerto Rican families (n = 157) that contained at least one parent with a substance use disorder to describe the impact of acculturation, parenting, and intimate partner violence on child behavioral issues. Findings indicated that parental distress, parent–child dysfunctional interactions, and parental reinforcement had direct influences on child behavior problems for Puerto Ricans. Implications for social work practice are explored, such as an increased focus on the parenting experience, decreasing the stress of the parent, and increasing reinforcement of positive child behavior.

Parenting plays a crucial role in child development as both a risk and protective factor. For children exposed to multiple prolonged traumas such as substance use disorder (SUD) from either one or both parents and intimate partner violence (IPV), parenting can be disrupted. The body of literature on the effects of trauma for children related to IPV and exposure to SUD is growing, but lacks specificity to Latino populations and subgroups. In response to this paucity of knowledge, this article focuses on Puerto Rican families with a history of SUD to investigate the effects of trauma exposure (SUD and IPV) on child behavioral issues. Family factors such as parenting and acculturation are considered as potential areas for intervention and prevention.

SUBSTANCE USE AMONG LATINOS

The Latino population is now the largest minority group in the United States, and it is the fastest growing minority group, with an increase of 3.3% between 2007 and 2008 (U.S. Census Bureau, 2010). Higher substance use in the Latino population compared to non-Latinos has been well documented, however, subgroups of Latinos, particularly Puerto Ricans, have not been as well researched. Mexican American and Puerto Rican men report higher rates of alcohol abuse and dependence than Cuban, Dominican, or South and Central Americans compared to non-Latino men in the United States (Caetano, Ramisetty-Mikler, & Rodriguez, 2008; Grant et al., 2004). Middle-aged (40–49 and 50–59 years) Puerto Rican and Mexican American men are at considerably higher risk of alcohol dependence than men in the general population (Caetano, Ramisetty-Mikler, & Rodriguez, 2008). Further, alcohol abuse and dependence rates are higher among U.S.-born Puerto Ricans and Dominicans than their foreign-born counterparts, but no such difference was found for Cuban and Mexican Americans (Caetano, Ramisetty-Mikler, & Rodriguez, 2008). Overall, those with higher acculturation report higher rates of substance abuse and dependence (statistically significant only for abuse among Puerto Ricans; Ramisetty-Mikler, Caetano, & Rodriguez, 2010). Injection drug use has also been found to be higher among Puerto Ricans than any other Latino subgroup (Kang, Deren, Andia, Colon, & Robles, 2001). The lack of literature on Puerto Rican substance use has prevented the expansion of knowledge on the effects of substance use on Puerto Rican families and children.

INTIMATE PARTNER VIOLENCE AMONG LATINOS

The Family Violence Prevention Fund (2008) defines IPV as physical, sexual, or psychological harm by a current or former intimate partner or spouse; it includes a pattern of coercive or manipulative behaviors perpetrated by one intimate partner against the other to gain or maintain control in the relationship. Findings from national surveys indicate that approximately one in five women is physically assaulted by a current or former partner during her lifetime (Tjaden & Thoennes, 2000a, 2000b). Research shows strong correlations between substance abuse and IPV (Call & Nelsen, 2007; Wekerle & Wall, 2002; Wilson-Cohn, Strauss, & Falkin, 2002). Women whose male partners had drug or alcohol problems, or those who reported that both they and their partners had a drug or alcohol problem, were also at increased risk for IPV (Coker, Smith, Bethea, King, & McKeown, 2000).

The literature on the relationship between partner violence and ethnic background is sparse and nonspecific to Latino subgroups. Many researchers have focused on IPV in Latino families because of a presumed higher level of male dominance in those families, a stereotype that a number of empirical studies have disproved (Straus & Smith, 1990). Descriptive findings from national studies have shown Latinos to have higher domestic violence rates (Tjaden & Thoennes, 2000a, 2000b). However, researchers who have controlled for socioeconomic factors found that differences were no longer statistically significant (Kaufman Kantor, Jasinski, & Aldarondo, 1994). The presence of interpersonal violence and trauma in the lives of women with cooccurring substance abuse and mental health problems is well established (Chilcoat & Menard, 2003; Najavits, Weiss, & Shaw, 1997). These stressors result in the development of distress that is manifest in symptoms of traumatic stress, depression, or the development of full-blown posttraumatic stress disorder (PTSD) or other disorders (Gatz et al., 2005; Salasin, 2005; Stewart & Conrod, 2003). These symptoms affect individuals' functioning in their parenting and social roles and can increase their use of substances.

INTIMATE PARTNER VIOLENCE EFFECTS ON CHILDREN

Children are significantly overrepresented in homes in which IPV occurs (Fantuzzo, Boruch, Beriama, Atkins, & Marcus, 1997). For example, Rennison (2003) reported that almost half of all incidents of IPV occurred in homes with a child under the age of 12, reflecting approximately 297,435 children in 1 year who were exposed to IPV. Children exposed to parental violence are also frequently the victims of child maltreatment and poor parenting practices such as verbal abuse and physical punishment (Kerker, Horwitz, Leventhal, Plichta, & Leaf, 2000; Tajima, 2000). Witnessing IPV between caregivers is a particular type of trauma for a child that could have devastating effects on development and can be a threat to children's sense of security and well-being, which influences all domains of development (Pepler, Catallo, & Moore, 2000).

Predictable, sensitive, and responsive caregiving during times of stress is crucial for optimal child development. Children who hear or see unresolved angry conflict or witness a parent being hurt could show symptoms of PTSD, including eating problems, sleep disturbances, lack of typical responses to adults, and loss of previously acquired developmental skills (Bogat, DeJonghe, Levendosky, Davidson, & von Eye, 2006; De Bellis & Thomas, 2003; Schore, 2001). Scheeringa and Zeanah (1995) suggested that threat to a caregiver could be one of the most psychologically destructive traumas for young children.

PARENTING AND IPV

Not all children exposed to IPV will exhibit trauma symptoms. Research suggests that there is variability in the emotional and behavioral outcomes of children exposed to IPV. An explanation for the range of observed outcomes includes the degree to which IPV impacts the parenting relationship. A large body of literature on nonmaltreating families suggests that parenting, including maternal sensitivity, mental health, and stress, impacts children's attachment and behavior (McKelvey, Fitzgerald, Schiffman, & von Eye, 2002; Pilowsky et al., 2006). For example, Graham-Bermann and Levendosky (1998) found a significant relationship between experiencing IPV and parenting stress, which was further related to parenting and child outcomes. In this study women who were experiencing more severe violence reported increased stress, which impacted internalizing and externalizing behavior in their school-aged children beyond the effects of the violence alone (Graham-Bermann & Levendosky, 1998). Huth-Bocks and Hughes (2008) also found that there was an interrelationship between parenting stress and ineffective parenting; however, contrary to the findings of others, this study did not find that severity of IPV was associated with parenting stress.

CULTURAL INFLUENCES AND ACCULTURATION

Puerto Ricans are the second largest group of Latinos in the United States (Oropesa, Landale, & Greif, 2008). There are several cultural constructs that have described Latino and Puerto Rican families such as *familismo, simpatia, personalismo, respeto, machismo,* and *marianismo* (Arcia, Reyes-Blanes, & Vazquez-Montilla, 2000; Calzada & Eyberg, 2002; Ortiz-Torres, Serrano-Garcia, & Torres-Burgos, 2000). These typical cultural values frame parenting in Puerto Rican families and have a direct impact on the family's sense of control over life events and hardships, parental reinforcement, and monitoring. In addition, parental stress and dysfunctional parent–child interactions exist in any family model but are exasperated by the traumatic environment of a household with one or more parents with an SUD.

Acculturation is the process by which migrant groups adapt their behaviors as they interact with the mainstream culture (Rogler, Cortes, &

Malgady, 1991). Acculturation has also been found to be a risk marker, with U.S.-born Mexican Americans and U.S. mainland-born Puerto Ricans having higher partner violence rates than their counterparts who are born in Mexico or born on the island of Puerto Rico (Kaufman Kantor et al., 1994; Sorenson & Telles, 1991). The research on ethnic influences on IPV is difficult to interpret because many studies have treated Latinos as a homogenous category (Kaufman Kantor et al., 1994). Kaufman Kantor et al. (1994) found considerable variation in marital violence rates, norms toward violence, and other related factors among Latino subgroups, suggesting that the lack of specificity in defining ethnicity as well as considering migration patterns and degree of acculturation might be serious shortcomings.

Acculturation dynamics, such as changing gender roles and expectations and acculturative stress, have been associated with higher incidence of IPV among Latinas (Harris, Firestone, & Vega, 2005; Jasinski, 1998). Some studies have found that the more traditional the orientation (i.e., strong *familismo* and strict gender roles) among Latina women, the less likely they are to report IPV (Harris et al., 2005). Researchers have identified some factors that increase the susceptibility of Latinos to IPV: immigration (Aldarondo, Kaufman Kantor, & Jasinski, 2002), acculturation (Caetano et al., 2007; Jasinski, 1998), socioeconomic deprivation and stressors (Kaufman Kantor et al., 1994), cultural gender factors such as *machismo* and *marianismo* (Moreno, 2007), and the presence of alcohol and drug use (Caetano et al., 2007; Neff, Holamon, & Davis Schlüter, 1995).

Social networks could provide additional contexts that affect IPV. A social network is known to provide one with comfort and security (Hirsch, 1981; Lin & Peek, 1999). The presence of a social network to provide social or emotional support to the individual or family can be important for Latino families; however, often a social network can lead to increased exposure and support of IPV (Barnett, Martinez, & Keyson, 1996; Coohey, 2007). Social networks also seem to affect perpetration. The lack of a social network tends to lead to high levels of stress, which are often reported to increase the risk for IPV perpetration (Tolman & Bennett, 1990). This seems to be particularly true for ethnic minorities, who might experience the loss of the social networks they had in their home countries (Kim, Lau, & Chang, 2006). The risk for IPV increases in neighborhoods characterized by poverty and associated with community violence and crime (Benson, Fox, DeMaris, & Van Wyk, 2003; Renzetti & Maier, 2002). Understanding gender roles in Puerto Rican families and support networks, such as the machismo and marianismo roles, might cause relationships to interact in different ways across different cultural contexts (Sarkisian & Gerstel, 2004). Furthermore, social support selection and affiliation in U.S. minority cultures is likely to be influenced not only by the availability of potential social support members, but also by shared ethnicity (McPherson, Smith-Lovin, & Cook, 2001).

This study examined Puerto Rican families that contain at least one parent with an SUD to describe the impact of acculturation, parenting, and IPV on child behavioral issues. The research objectives for this study were to (a) describe this sample of Puerto Rican substance-using families; (b) examine the bivariate relationships between parenting attributes or behaviors, IPV, and child behavioral outcomes; and (c) examine the unique contributions of these parenting behaviors to child behavioral outcomes. Protective factors such as the strengths of the family and strong connections to the Latino culture were explored in relationship to child behavioral problems in a traumatic environment. Direct suggestions for social workers on strengthening and preserving family factors in at-risk communities are highlighted.

METHODOLOGY

Participants

This article utilizes data from the Latino Family Connection Project, a culturally adapted Strengthening Families Program (Chartier, Negroni, & Hesselbrock, 2010). For the purposes of this study, only the Puerto Rican families have been selected and all the measures are taken from surveys given at baseline. Puerto Rican families from two urban centers in Connecticut participated in the study. All families had to have a child age 9 to 12 and a parent who had either received substance abuse treatment or had a documented SUD. A total of 157 Puerto Rican parent–youth dyads participated.

Procedures

Families were recruited through presentations, and brochures and flyers distributed by primarily bilingual program staff. Churches, elementary schools, family courts and resource centers, mental health agencies, alcohol and drug treatment facilities, and youth service bureaus were contacted to serve as referral sources to the project. Families received an incentive for completing the research interviews consisting of $25 for the baseline interviews. All forms had identification numbers and no identifiable data were gathered, and confidentiality of all participants was maintained by training all staff on institutional review board guidelines. All surveys were available in Spanish. All research procedures were approved by the University of Connecticut Institutional Review Board.

Variables and Measures

The study examined the impact of parenting, family and cultural factors (acculturation), and social networks on children behavioral issues in families that had been exposed to both SUD and IPV. Parenting was measured by examining parental reinforcement, parental monitoring, and parenting stress. Acculturation included parents' place of birth, cultural connections, and support network.

Intimate partner violence

The parent or caregiver completed three items asking if his or her spouse or partner ever abused him or her emotionally, physically, or sexually. A sum of the three items provided a total abuse score ranging from no abuse to high levels of abuse. For this study the IPV measure had a good internal consistency ($\alpha = .72$).

Child behavioral issues

Child behavioral issues were measured by the Parent Observation of Children's Activities (POCA–R) created by Kellam (1990) at Johns Hopkins University. This standardized test is a modification of the Child Behavior Checklist (CBCL; Achenbach & Edelbrock, 1983) to be more sensitive to change. The POCA–R uses less clinical wording compared to the CBCL to be more acceptable to parents and to improve parent understanding of the constructs measured. The POCA–R has been used to measure child behavior change in relation to interventions for child substance use prevention. The POCA–R has also been used in samples of mostly urban children to investigate the effects of family structure on child behavior (Pearson, Ialongo, Hunter, & Kellam, 1994). The POCA–R has been used in various Strengthening Families Programs (SFPs) and is an intervention listed on the Substance Abuse and Mental Health Services Administration (SAMHSA) national registry for evidence-based programs. The SFP focuses on the prevention of problems in children of substance-abusing parents (Kumpfer, 1998; Kumpfer & Alverado, 1998) and has been used with different ethnic and racial groups (Kumpfer, Alvarado, Smith, & Bellamy, 2002). Kumpfer, Alvarado, Tait, and Turner (2002) found improvement in child behavior issues, as measured by the POCA–R, as a result of a combined intervention focusing on family and school environment. Six child negative outcomes were measured: child overt and covert aggression, depression, hyperactivity, concentration problems, and criminal behavior. A total scale mean score ranges from 1 to 4 with higher numbers indicating more behavioral issues. For this study the POCA–R had a good internal consistency ($\alpha = .90$).

Parental reinforcement

The parent or caregiver answered three questions on the types of reinforcement given to the child, such as how often they use verbal punishment, how often they use praise for desired behavior, and how often they tell their child they are doing a good job. Response options ranged from *never* to *daily or more than once per day*, with a total of five options. Total scores ranged from 5 to 15, with low numbers indicating less positive parental reinforcement and higher numbers indicating positive parental reinforcement.

Parental monitoring

Parental monitoring was assessed by asking the parent or caregiver eight questions on knowing child's friends, knowing what their child was doing, how much time they spent with the child, and curfew expectations. The eight items were based on a five-option response scale, ranging from 1 (*low parental monitoring*) to 5 (*high parental monitoring*).

Parenting stress

Two subscales from the Parenting Stress Index–Short Form (PSI–SF; Abidin, 1995) were administered to parents or caregivers: (a) The *parental distress* scale assesses each parent or caregiver's level of distress in his or her role as a parent; and (b) the *parent–child dysfunctional interaction* scale measures the parent or caregiver's perceptions of parent–child estrangement. Each subscale contains 12 items and ranges in score from 12 to 60, with higher scores indicating greater levels of stress or dysfunction. The parenting stress scale has a good internal consistency (α = .91).

Family hardiness

Parents and caregivers completed the 20-item Family Hardiness Index (FHI; McCubbin & Thompson, 1991). Hardiness is characterized by a family's sense of control over life events and hardships. The total scale was summed after reverse-scoring. The FHI has good internal consistency with an alpha of .82 (Fischer & Corcoran, 2007), and an alpha of .80 for this study

Acculturation: Place of birth, cultural connections, and social network

Place of birth was asked of the parent or caregiver: either Puerto Rico or U.S. mainland. Cultural connections were measured by the amount of contact the parent or caregiver reported with Puerto Ricans and Latinos. Three questions were asked about the type of food they preferred, who lived in their neighborhood, and from whom they get most of their social support. Options included from mostly Anglos, both or a mixture, and mostly

Puerto Ricans and Latinos. Responses were summed and range from 9 to 5, with higher numbers indicating more Puerto Rican and Latino contact (lower acculturation) and lower numbers indicating more Anglo contact (higher acculturation). Social network was measured by asking the parents or caregivers about the sources of social or emotional support available to their family. The scale contained six items asking about family, close friends, spiritual community, neighbors, social workers, and support groups like Alcoholics Anonymous or Narcotics Anonymous, with higher scores indicating more social support.

FINDINGS

Characteristics of the study sample measured at baseline are provided in Table 1. All parent and caregiver respondents were Puerto Rican, had a child age 9 to 12, and had either themselves (21%) or a partner (79%) who received substance abuse treatment or had a documented SUD.

Most of the parent respondents were female (91%), born in Puerto Rico (76%), had three children, averaged 36 years of age old, and had on average 10.25 years of education. The children averaged 10 years of age, and over half (51%) were girls. The parent who filled out the survey had high levels of experiencing IPV, with 64% experiencing emotional abuse, 44% physical abuse, and 20% sexual abuse.

Table 2 provides a correlation matrix on the parent, family, and social indicators utilized for prediction of child behavioral problems. Significant

TABLE 1 Demographic Characteristics of Puerto Rican Families

Demographics	*M* or %
Parent or caregiver	
Age	36.43 (± 9.72)
Education in years	10.25 (± 2.88)
No. of children	3.22 (± 1.43)
% female	91%
Place of birth (%)	
U.S. mainland	24%
Puerto Rico	76%
% treated for SUD	21%
% spouse treated for SUD	79%
Intimate partner violence (%)	
Emotional abuse	64%
Physical abuse	44%
Sexual abuse	20%
Child	
Age	10.23 (± 1.24)
% female	51%

Notes. $N = 157$. SUD = substance use disorder.

TABLE 2 Correlation Matrix of Parent, Family, and Social Indicators

	1	2	3	4	5	6	7	8	9	10
Intimate partner violence (1)	1	.101	−.036	−.121	.158*	.023	−.053	.016	.121	.143
Social network (2)		1	.084	−.146	−.087	−.084	.040	−.212*	.088	.044
Family hardiness (3)			1	.254*	−.345*	−.330*	.022	.016	−.086	−.232*
Parental monitoring (4)				1	−.134	−.277*	.135	.039	−.132	−.212*
Parental distress (5)					1	.603*	−.199*	.040	−.037	.441*
Parent–child dysfunction (6)						1	−.254*	−.057	−.061	.479*
Parenting reinforcement (7)							1	−.161	−.073	−.375*
Cultural connections (8)								1	−.101	.151
Place of birth (1 = U.S., 0 = Puerto Rico) (9)									1	.076
Child behavioral issues (10)										1

*Correlation significant at $p < .05$ level.

correlations exist between family hardiness, parental monitoring, parental distress, and parent and youth interaction. Also apparent is the significant correlation between IPV and parental distress.

Standard multiple regression was used to assess the effects of exposure to IPV and family protective factors (family hardiness, parental monitoring, parental reinforcement) and parenting stressors (parental distress, parent–child dysfunctional interactions) in the context of acculturation (place born, cultural connections, and social network) on the ability to predict child behavioral problems. Using the recommendations of Tabachnick and Fidell (2007) for adequate sample size using number of independent variables ($N > 50 + 8$ (number of independent variables) $= N$ must be larger than 122), this sample of 157 Puerto Rican families is adequate for this analysis. Preliminary analyses were conducted to ensure no violation of the assumptions of normality, linearity, multicollinearity, and homoscedasticity.

The total variance explained by the model as a whole was 38.3%, $F(9, 126) = 8.70, p < .001$. In the model, nine independent variables were entered and all standardized and unstandardized betas are presented in Table 3.

Five independent variables contributed significantly to child behavioral problems: two acculturation measures and three parenting measures. Parent–child dysfunctional interaction was statistically significant with the highest standardized beta value ($\beta = .308, p = .001$). Parental reinforcement was inversely related to child behavior problems ($\beta = -.226, p = .003$). Parental distress also significantly predicted child behavioral problems ($\beta = .184, p = .047$). Two acculturation measures, cultural connections and social networks, were significant predictors of child behavior problems ($\beta = .165, p = .027$, and $\beta = .146, p = .050$, respectively). Both measures were related positively, with more social networks and more cultural connections the more reported

TABLE 3 Multiple Regression Analysis of the Effects of Intimate Partner Violence, Family, and Acculturation Factors on Child Behavior Problems for Puerto Rican Families

	Unstandardized Coefficients		Standardized Coefficients	Significance Level
	B	*SE*	β	
Intimate partner violence	.021	.024	.064	.380
Parental reinforcement	−.041	.014	−.226	.003**
Family hardiness	−.003	.003	−.063	.423
Parental monitoring	−.303	.101	−.023	.764
Parental distress	.008	.004	.184	.047*
Parent–child dysfunction	.014	.004	.308	.001**
Place born	.064	.063	.073	.315
Cultural connections	.063	.028	.165	.027*
Social network	.041	.021	.146	.050*

Note. $N = 157$.
*$p \le .05$. **$p \le .01$.

child behavior problems. Multinomial logistic regression was conducted to determine if parenting, family, and acculturation factors predicted IPV, but the model was not significant.

DISCUSSION

The importance of parenting on the effects of child behavior problems in traumatic environments found in this study is consistent with the literature (McKelvey et al., 2002; Pilowsky et al., 2006). This study found that high levels of parenting distress and high levels of parent–child dysfunctional interactions predicted more child behavior problems. In addition, parental reinforcement led to fewer child behavior problems. As Graham-Bermann and Levendosky (1998) found, parents who are involved in IPV situations experience greater parental distress. This study demonstrates that parental distress has a direct influence on child behavior problems for Puerto Rican children. There was also a positive relationship between IPV and parental distress, indicating that for families with high levels of IPV there were high levels of parental distress. However, given the correlational relationship it is impossible to determine if IPV or parental distress occurred first in the order of events.

Perhaps the most complex findings are the significant relationships between high levels of cultural connections and social networks related to more child behavior problems. These findings indicate that more contact with Latinos and Puerto Ricans through contact in the neighborhood and social support predicts greater child behavior problems. These findings are contrary to findings on low levels of acculturation functioning as a protective mechanism for Latino families related to health and behavior outcomes (Duncan, Hotz, & Trejo, 2006; Grogger & Trejo, 2002; Zsembik & Fennell, 2005). In addition, these findings are in conflict with the findings of previous studies suggesting that Latino culture exerts protective effects through high *familismo* and strong social bonds (Gloria & Peregoy, 1996; Marsiglia, Kulis, Nieri, & Parsai, 2005; Parsai, Voisine, Marsiglia, Kulis, & Nieri, 2009). However, the findings in the literature are of either Latinos as a large group or of Mexican Americans. Also, there is a possibility that maintaining strong cultural bonds might limit parents from understanding, accepting, and coping with their children's acculturation processes, thus contributing to more parent–child conflicts. Affiliating with delinquent peers or social networks has been found to increase the risk for perpetrating violence against an intimate in studies across disciplines (DeKeseredy & Schwartz, 1998; Silverman & Williamson, 1997). Social learning theories (Akers, 1977; Bandura, 1973; Burgess & Akers, 1966) provide a framework for understanding how violent behavior toward women might be learned and legitimized within such social support networks (Silverman & Williamson, 1997). This hypothesis needs to be examined empirically. We found no recent research looking specifically at acculturation and Puerto Rican substance users and IPV.

One aspect of acculturation, *familismo,* is often defined as family support, connections among family members, perceptions of the family as a behavioral and attitudinal referent, family honor, and feeling obligated toward one's family (Lugo Steidel & Contreras, 2003; Sabogal, Marín, Otero-Sabogal, & VanOss Marín, 1987). Research on families with IPV and SUD indicates that often the family and social network connections might be with members who support their drug use or do not interfere with the violence dynamic (Havassy, Hall, & Wasserman, 1991; Hunter-Reel, McCrady, & Hildebrandt, 2009). Given the framework of the Latino family and the specifics of substance use and IPV, the findings of this study are more interpretable. Perhaps the high levels of ethnic social relations and networks are with other substance-using family and community members and these are negatively affecting child behavior problems and the family.

The research on Puerto Rican families experiencing IPV and SUD is sparse, making the interpretation of these findings difficult. Given the evidence for the negative effects of witnessing or exposure to IPV on all aspects of a child's well-being (Pepler et al., 2000), the study findings reported here are interesting. In this study, IPV did not significantly predict child behavior problems. Various reasons could account for this finding; one potential reason is the resilience of Puerto Rican families and children to withstand the effects of exposure to IPV and SUD. Resilience is a process that involves exposure to risk or serious threats, yet results in successful outcomes and a positive adjustment despite these experiences of adversity (Luthar & Cicchetti, 2000; Masten et al., 1999). A focus on resiliency within the Latino community continues to be established; however, there are few models that indicate how to work with Latino clients that are focused on resiliency (Mogro-Wilson, 2011). Also, cultural values such as *familismo, marianismo,* and *respeto* might have a protective influence on the exercise of the parental responsibilities specifically for the mother (91% of the sample) and help protect children from developing behavioral difficulties.

Another possibility is that exposure to IPV is affecting the parenting process, parental stress and reinforcement, and the child–parent interactions, similar to findings of Graham-Bermann and Levendosky (1998), who found a significant relationship between experiencing IPV and parenting stress. Further exploration into the study's model, perhaps utilizing structural equation modeling, if sample size would allow, would provide insight into mediating and moderating variables and could give more information on the effects of IPV for Puerto Rican families.

All families involved in this study had at least one parent with an SUD, and IPV was highly prevalent, all risk factors of child behavioral issues. However, protective factors such as the family and parenting were very important to these at-risk families. The findings on parental distress and parent–child dysfunctional interactions are promising for intervention and prevention in Puerto Rican families and can be addressed in clinical and family therapy models. Providers working with children in families exposed to multiple traumas might choose to focus on parenting reinforcement practices such as praising the child for desired behaviors, or reminding parents to tell their children they are doing a good job. Relieving parental distress through group work with other parents in similar situations might prove a useful technique (Peled, Davidson-Arad, & Perel, 2010). Prevention of child difficulties could focus on creating and providing opportunities and resources geared at decreasing those major contributing factors to Puerto Rican parents' (mothers') distress. Further research that explores the realities and challenges faced by Puerto Rican mothers could help understand ways in which these mothers' level of distress can be reduced. Likewise, further research should explore the factors that decrease parent–child interactions. Concerns have been raised regarding the impact of experiences of acculturation within the family and how different levels of acculturation among family members might be conducive to conflictive parent–child interactions.

Limitations

There are various limitations of this study, such as the small sample size and nonrandom methods of sampling, that limit the implications for generalization. In addition, the cross-sectional design allows for correlational and noncausal results. The specific measures chosen for acculturation are incomplete and further specification of acculturation in a multidimensional model is necessary. The lack of detailed information on IPV, such as how old the child was when exposed to the violence or the severity of the violence, limits the understating of the influence of IPV on child behavioral issues. IPV was not defined, and the respondents were asked if they ever experienced physical abuse, emotional abuse, or sexual abuse. Because cultures define abuse in different ways, such varying definitions could contribute to the findings. It is possible the findings related to IPV might be due to the format of the questions, which asked about lifetime IPV experience, and not necessarily recent abuse. In addition, investigating families and children exposed to trauma is complex and the numerous factors involved in the development of child behavior problems in this context make it necessary to limit the constructs in prediction; however, this restricts the understanding of the family and child as a unit.

CONCLUSION

This study makes a contribution to the literature by investigating the effects of parenting and acculturation on Puerto Rican children in traumatic home environments exposed to SUD and IPV. It provides preliminary evidence of the importance of parenting practices and the potential effects of negative social networks and ethnic social relations for child behavior problems. The importance for social work practice to focus on the parenting experience, the interactions between the parent and the child, the stress of the parent, and how the parent reinforces positive behavior has strong influences on child behavior problems in traumatic family environments. In addition, social work practice should continue to focus on the type of ethnic relationship and social networks maintained by the family to investigate the potential damaging effects on continued exposure to substance use and possible supportive behavior toward IPV. More research on Puerto Rican families, the cultural and family factors associated with child outcomes affected by SUD and IPV, is necessary and would allow for further interpretation of these results.

REFERENCES

Abidin, R. R. (1995). *Parenting stress index: Professional manual* (Vol. 3). Odessa, FL: Psychological Assessment Resources.

Achenbach, T. M., & Edelbrock, C. S. (1983). *Manual for the child behavior checklist and revised behavior profile*. Burlington, VT: University of Vermont Department of Psychiatry.

Akers, R. L. (1977). Type of leadership in prison: A structural approach to testing the functional and importation models. *Sociological Quarterly, 18*, 378–383.

Aldarondo, E., Kaufman Kantor, G., & Jasinski, J. L. (2002). A risk marker analysis of wife assault in Latino families. *Violence Against Women, 5*, 429–454.

Arcia, E., Reyes-Blanes, M. E., & Vazquez-Montilla, E. (2000). Constructions and reconstructions: Latino parents' values for children. *Journal of Child and Family Studies, 9*(3), 333–350.

Bandura, A. (1973). *Aggression: A social learning analysis*. Oxford, UK: Prentice Hall.

Barnett, O. W., Martinez, T. E., & Keyson, M. (1996). The relationship between violence, social support, and self-blame in battered women. *Journal of Interpersonal Violence, 11*, 221–233.

Benson, M., Fox, G. L., DeMaris, A., & Van Wyk, J. (2003). Neighborhood disadvantage, individual economic distress and violence against women in intimate relationships. *Journal of Quantitative Criminology, 19*, 207–234.

Bogat, G. A., DeJonghe, E., Levendosky, A. A., Davidson, W. S., & von Eye, A. (2006). Trauma symptoms among infants exposed to intimate partner violence. *Child Abuse and Neglect, 30*, 109–125.

Burgess, R. L., & Akers, R. L. (1966). Are operant principles tautological? *Psychological Record, 16*, 305–312.

Caetano, R., Ramisetty-Mikler, S., Caetano, P. A., & Harris, J. R. (2007). Acculturation stress, drinking and intimate partner violence among Hispanic couples in the U.S. *Journal of Interpersonal Violence, 22*, 1431–1447.

Caetano, R., Ramisetty-Mikler, S., & Rodriguez, L. A. (2008). The Hispanic Americans Baseline Alcohol Survey (HABLAS): Rates and predictors of alcohol abuse and dependence across Hispanic national groups. *Journal of Studies on Alcohol and Drugs*, *69*, 441–448.

Call, C. R., & Nelsen, J. C. (2007). Partner abuse and women's substance problems: From vulnerability to strength. *Affilia: Journal of Women and Social Work*, *22*, 334–346.

Calzada, E. J., & Eyberg, S. M. (2002). Self-reported parenting practices in Dominican and Puerto Rican mothers of young children. *Journal of Clinical Child and Adolescent Psychology*, *3*, 354–363.

Chartier, K. G., Negroni, L. N., & Hesselbrock, M. N. (2010). Strengthening family practices for Latino families. *Journal of Ethnic and Cultural Diversity in Social Work*, *19*, 1–17.

Chilcoat, H. D., & Menard, C. (2003). Epidemiological investigations: Comorbidity of posttraumatic stress disorder and substance use disorder. In P. Ouimette & P. J. Brown (Eds.), *Trauma and substance abuse* (pp. 9–29). Washington, DC: American Psychological Association.

Coker, A. L., Smith, P. H., Bethea, L., King, M. R., & McKeown, R. E. (2000). Physical health consequences of physical and psychological intimate partner violence. *Archives of Family Medicine*, *9*, 451–457.

Coohey, C. (2007). The relationship between mothers' social networks and severe domestic violence: A test of the social isolation hypothesis. *Violence and Victims*, *22*, 503–512.

De Bellis, M. D., & Thomas, L. A. (2003). Biological findings of post-traumatic stress disorder and child maltreatment. *Current Psychiatry Reports*, *5*, 108–117.

DeKeseredy, W. S., & Schwartz, M. D. (1998). Male peer support and woman abuse in postsecondary school courtship: Suggestions for new directions in sociological research. In R. K. Bergen (Ed.), *Issues in intimate violence* (pp. 83–96). Thousand Oaks, CA: Sage.

Duncan, B., Hotz, V. J., & Trejo, S. J. (2006). Hispanics in the U.S. labor market. In National Research Council (Ed.), *Hispanics and the future of America* (pp. 228–290). Washington, DC: National Academies Press.

Family Violence Prevention Fund. (2008). *Get the facts: Domestic violence is a serious, widespread social problem in America: The facts*. Retrieved from http://www.endabuse.org/userfiles/file/Children_and_Families/DomesticViolence.pdf

Fantuzzo, J., Boruch, R., Beriama, A., Atkins, M., & Marcus, S. (1997). Domestic violence and children: Prevalence and risk in five major US cities. *Journal of the American Academy of Child and Adolescent Psychiatry*, *36*(1), 116–122.

Fischer, J., & Corcoran, K. J. (2007). *Measures for clinical practice and research: A sourcebook* (Vol. 1, 4th ed.). New York, NY: Oxford University Press.

Gatz, M., Russell, L., Grady, J., Kram-Fernandez, D., Clark, C., & Marshall, B. (2005). Women's recollections of victimization, psychological problems, and substance use. *Journal of Community Psychology*, *33*, 379–393.

Gloria, A. M., & Peregoy, J. J. (1996). Counseling Latino alcohol and other substance users/abusers: Cultural considerations for counselors. *Journal of Substance Abuse Treatment*, *13*, 119–126.

Graham-Bermann, S. A., & Levendosky, A. A. (1998). Traumatic stress symptoms in children of battered women. *Journal of Interpersonal Violence*, *13*(1), 111–128.

Grant, B. F., Dawson, D. A., Stinson, F. S., Chou, S. P., Dufour, M. C., & Pickering, R. C. (2004). The 12-month prevalence and trends in DSM–IV alcohol abuse and dependence: United States, 1991–1992 and 2001–2002. *Drug Alcohol Dependence, 74*, 223–234.

Grogger, J., & Trejo, S. J. (2002). *Falling behind or moving up? The intergenerational progress of Mexican Americans*. San Francisco, CA: Public Policy Institute of California.

Harris, R., Firestone, J., & Vega, W. (2005). The interaction of country of origin, acculturation and gender role ideology on wife abuse. *Social Science Quarterly, 86*, 463–483.

Havassy, B. E., Hall, S. M., & Wasserman, D. A. (1991). Social support and relapse: Commonalities among alcoholics, opiate users and cigarette smokers. *Addiction Behavior, 61*, 235–246.

Hirsch, B. J. (1981). Social networks and the coping process: Creating personal communities. In B. H. Gottlieb (Ed.), *Social networks and social support* (pp. 149–170). Beverly Hills, CA: Sage.

Hunter-Reel, D., McCrady, B., & Hildebrandt, T. (2009). Emphasizing interpersonal factors: An extension of the Witkiewitz and Marlatt relapse model. *Addiction, 104*(8), 1281–1290.

Huth-Bocks, A. C., & Hughes, H. M. (2008). Parenting stress, parenting behavior, and children's adjustment in families experiencing intimate partner violence. *Journal of Family Violence, 23*, 243–251.

Jasinski, J. L. (1998). The role of acculturation in wife assault. *Hispanic Journal of Behavioral Sciences, 20*, 175–191.

Kang, S. Y., Deren, S., Andia, J., Colon, H., & Robles, R. (2001). Gender differences in HIV risk behaviors among Puerto Rican drug injectors by awareness of HIV seropositive status. *AIDS & Behavior, 5*, 241–249.

Kaufman Kantor, G., Jasinski, J. L., & Aldarondo, E. (1994). Sociocultural status and incidence of marital violence in Hispanic families. *Violence and Victims, 9*(3), 207–222.

Kellam, S. G. (1990). Developmental epidemiologic framework for family research on depression and aggression. In G. R. Patterson (Ed.), *Depression and aggression in family interaction* (pp. 11–48). Hillsdale, NJ: Erlbaum.

Kerker, B. D., Horwitz, S. M., Leventhal, J. M., Plichta, S., & Leaf, P. J. (2000). Identification of violence in the home: Pediatric and parental reports. *Archives of Pediatrics and Adolescent Medicine, 154*, 457–462.

Kim, I. J., Lau, A. S., & Chang, D. F. (2006). Family violence. In F. T. Leong, A. G. Inman, A. Ebreo, L. Yang, L. M. Kinoshita, & M. Fu (Eds.), *Handbook of Asian American psychology* (pp. 363–378). Thousand Oaks, CA: Sage.

Kumpfer, K. L. (1998). The strengthening families program. In R. S. Ashery, E. Robertson, & K. L. Kumpfer (Eds.), *Drug abuse prevention through family interventions* (NIDA Research Monograph No. 177, pp. 160–207). Rockville, MD: National Institute on Drug Abuse.

Kumpfer, K. L., & Alvarado, R. (1998). Effective family strengthening interventions. *Juvenile Justice Bulletin* (Pub. No. NCJ 171121). Washington, DC: Office of Juvenile Justice and Delinquency Prevention, U.S. Department of Justice.

Kumpfer, K. L., Alvarado, R., Smith, P., & Bellamy, N. (2002). Cultural sensitivity and adaptation in family-based prevention interventions. *Prevention Science, 3*(3), 241–246.

Kumpfer, K. L., Alvarado, R., Tait, C., & Turner, C. (2002). Effectiveness of school-based family and children's skills training for substance prevention among 6–8-year-old rural children. *Psychology of Addictive Behaviors, 16*(4), S65–S71.

Lin, N., & Peek, M. K. (1999). Social networks and mental health. In A. V. Horwitz & T. L. Sheid (Eds.), *A handbook for the study of mental health: Social contexts, theories, and systems* (pp. 241–258). New York, NY: Cambridge University Press.

Lugo Steidel, A. G., & Contreras, J. M. (2003). A new familism scale for use with Latino populations. *Hispanic Journal of Behavioral Sciences, 25*, 312–330.

Luthar, S. S., & Cicchetti, D. (2000). The construct of resilience: Implications for interventions and social policies. *Development and Psychopathology, 12*(4), 857–885.

Marsiglia, F. F., Kulis, S., Nieri, T., & Parsai, M. (2005). God forbid! Substance use among religious and non-religious youth. *The American Journal of Orthopsychiatry, 75*(4), 585–598.

Masten, A., Hubbard, J., Gest, S., Tellegen, A., Garmezy, N., & Ramirez, M. (1999). Competence in the context of adversity: Pathways to resilience and maladaptation from childhood to late adolescence. *Development and Psychopathology, 11*(1), 143–169.

McCubbin, H. I., & Thompson, A. I. (1991). *Family assessment inventories for research and practice*. Madison, WI: University of Wisconsin Press.

McKelvey, L., Fitzgerald, H., Schiffman, R., & von Eye, A. (2002). Family stress and parent–infant interaction: The mediating role of coping. *Infant Mental Health Journal, 23*(1/2), 164–181.

McPherson, M., Smith-Lovin, L., & Cook, J. M. (2001). Birds of a feather: Homophily in social networks. *Annual Review of Sociology, 27*, 415–444.

Mogro-Wilson, C. (2011). Resilience in vulnerable and at risk Latino families. *Infants and Young Children, 24*(3), 267–279.

Moreno, C. L. (2007). The relationship between culture, gender, structural factors, abuse, trauma, and HIV/ AIDS for Latinas. *Qualitative Health Research, 17*(3), 1–13.

Najavits, L. M., Weiss, R. D., & Shaw, S. R. (1997). The link between substance abuse and post-traumatic stress disorder in women: A research review. *American Journal on Addictions, 6*, 273–283.

Neff, J. A., Holamon, B., & Davis Schlüter, T. (1995). Spousal violence among Anglos, blacks, and Mexican Americans: The role of demographic variables, psychosocial predictors, and alcohol consumption. *Journal of Family Violence, 10*, 1–21.

Oropesa, R. S., Landale, N. S., & Greif, M. J. (2008). From Puerto Rican to pan-ethnic in New York City. *Ethnic and Racial Studies, 31*, 1315–1339.

Ortiz-Torres, B., Serrano-Garcia, L., & Torres-Burgos, N. (2000). Subverting culture: Promoting HIV/AIDS prevention among Puerto Rican and Dominican women. *Journal of Community Psychology, 28*, 859–881.

Parsai, M., Voisine, S., Marsiglia, F. F., Kulis, S., & Nieri, T. (2009). The protective and risk effects of parents and peers on substance use, attitudes and behaviors of Mexican and Mexican American female and male adolescents. *Youth and Society, 40*, 353–376.

Pearson, J. L., Ialongo, N. S., Hunter, A. G., & Kellam, S. G. (1994). Family structure and aggressive behavior in a population of urban elementary school children. *Journal of the American Academy of Child & Adolescent Psychiatry, 33*(4), 540–548.

Peled, E. E., Davidson-Arad, B. B., & Perel, G. G. (2010). The mothering of women abused by their partner: An outcome evaluation of a group intervention. *Research on Social Work Practice, 20*(4), 391–402.

Pepler, D. J., Catallo, R., & Moore, T. E. (2000). Consider the children: Research informing interventions for children exposed to domestic violence. *Journal of Aggression, Maltreatment, and Trauma, 3*(1), 37–57.

Pilowsky, D. J., Wickramaratne, P. J., Rush, D. J., Hughesm, C. W., Garber, J., Malloy, E., . . . Weissman, M. M. (2006). Children of currently depressed mothers: A STARD ancillary study. *Journal of Clinical Psychiatry, 67*(1), 126–136.

Ramisetty-Mikler, S., Caetano, R., & Rodriguez, L. A. (2010). The Hispanic Americans Baseline Alcohol Survey (HABLAS): Alcohol consumption and sociodemographic predictors across Hispanic national groups. *Journal of Substance Use, 15*(6), 402–416.

Rennison, C. M. (2003). *Intimate partner violence 1993–2001: Bureau of Justice Statistics crime data brief*. Washington, DC: U.S. Department of Justice.

Renzetti, C., & Maier, S. (2002). Private crime in public housing: Violent victimization, fear of crime and social isolation among women public housing residents. *Women's Health and Urban Life, 1*, 46–65.

Rogler, L. H., Cortes, D. E., & Malgady, R. (1991). Acculturation and mental health status among Hispanics: Convergence and new directions for research. *American Psychologist, 46*, 585–597.

Sabogal, F., Marín, G., Otero-Sabogal, R., & VanOss Marín, B. (1987). Hispanic familism and acculturation: What changes and what doesn't? *Hispanic Journal of Behavioral Sciences, 9*, 397–412.

Salasin, S. (2005). Evolution of women's trauma-integrated services at the Substance Abuse and Mental Health Services Administration. *Journal of Community Psychology, 33*, 379–393.

Sarkisian, N., & Gerstel, N. (2004). Kin support among Blacks and Whites: Race and family organization. *American Sociological Review, 69*, 812–837.

Scheeringa, M. S., & Zeanah, C. H. (1995). Symptom expression and trauma variables in children under 48 months of age. *Infant Mental Health Journal, 16*(4), 259–270.

Schore, A. N. (2001). The effects of early relational trauma on right brain development, affect regulation, and infant mental health. *Infant Mental Health Journal, 22*(1/2), 201 269.

Silverman, J. G., & Williamson, G. M. (1997). Social ecology and entitlements involved in battering by heterosexual college males: Contributions of family and peers. *Violence & Victims, 12*, 147–164.

Sorenson, S. B., & Telles, C. A. (1991). Self-reports of spousal violence in a Mexican-American and non-Hispanic white population. *Violence and Victims, 6*(1), 3–15.

Stewart, S. H., & Conrod, P. J. (2003). Psychosocial models of functional associations between posttraumatic stress disorder and substance use disorder. In

P. Ouimette & P. J. Brown (Eds.), *Trauma and substance abuse* (pp. 29–57). Washington, DC: American Psychological Association.

Straus, M. A., & Smith, C. (1990). Violence in Hispanic families in the United States: Incidence rates and structural interpretations. In M. A. Straus & R. J. Gelles (Eds.), *Physical violence in American families: Risk factors and adaptations to violence in 8,145 families* (pp. 341–368). New Brunswick, NJ: Transaction Books.

Tabachnick, B. G., & Fidell, L. S. (2007). *Using multivariate statistics* (5th ed.). Boston, MA: Allyn & Bacon.

Tajima, E. (2000). The relative importance of wife abuse as a risk factor for violence against children. *Child Abuse & Neglect, 24*(11), 1383–1398.

Tjaden, P., & Thoennes, N. (2000a). *Extent, nature, and consequences of intimate partner violence*. Washington, DC: U.S. Department of Justice, Office of Justice Programs.

Tjaden, P., & Thoennes, N. (2000b). *Full report of the prevalence, incidence, and consequences of violence against women*. Washington, DC: U.S. Department of Justice, National Institute of Justice.

Tolman, R. M., & Bennett, L. W. (1990). A review of quantitative research on men who batter. *Journal of Interpersonal Violence, 5*, 87–118.

U.S. Census Bureau. (2010). *U.S. Census brief*. Retrieved from http://www.census.gov/prod/cen2010/briefs/c2010br-02.pdf

Wekerle, C., & Wall, A. (2002). *The violence and addiction equation: Theoretical and clinical issues in substance abuse and relationship violence*. New York, NY: Brunner/Routledge.

Wilson-Cohn, C., Strauss, S. M., & Falkin, G. (2002). The relationship between partner abuse and substance use among women mandated to drug treatment. *Journal of Family Violence, 17*, 91–105.

Zsembik, B. A., & Fennell, D. (2005). Ethnic variation in health and the determinants of health among Latinos. *Social Science and Medicine, 61*, 53–63.

Caregiver Substance Abuse and Children's Exposure to Violence in a Nationally Representative Child Welfare Sample

KRISTEN D. SEAY, MSW
Doctoral Candidate, Brown School of Social Work, Washington University in St. Louis, St. Louis, Missouri, USA

PATRICIA L. KOHL, PhD
Associate Professor, Brown School of Social Work, Washington University in St. Louis, St. Louis, Missouri, USA

Using data from the National Survey of Child and Adolescent Well-Being II, this article examines the impact of caregiver substance abuse on children's exposure to violence in the home in a nationally representative sample of families involved with child protective services. Logistic regression analyses indicate an increased risk of witnessing mild and severe violence in the home for children whose primary caregiver was abusing alcohol or drugs. However, analyses did not find statistically significant relationships between child report of direct victimization in the home by mild or severe violence and caregiver alcohol or drug abuse.

With more than 1.5 million maltreatment reports assessed by child protective services (CPS) in 2010 (U.S. Department of Health and Human Services Administration for Children and Families, Administration on Children, Youth

Ms. Seay is supported by a National Institute on Drug Abuse Predoctoral Fellowship (#5T32DA015035) and a Doris Duke Fellowship. Support for this project was provided by the National Institute of Mental Health (R03MH082203).

and Families, Children's Bureau, 2011) and high rates of substance abuse among caregivers involved with child welfare, deepening our understanding of the impact of caregiver substance abuse on children's development and well-being is an important step in addressing the needs of the child welfare population. Although prevalence estimates vary greatly depending on sample characteristics, a general consensus is that between 50% and 80% of caregivers in the child welfare population are engaged in substance abuse (Besinger, Garland, Litrownik, & Landsverk, 1999; Jones, 2004; U.S. Government Accounting Office [GAO], 1994, 1998). The use of substances by a caregiver has been linked to negative outcomes for children and adolescents including substance use, eating disorders, teenage pregnancy, poor academic attendance and performance, and suicidality (Chandy, Blum, & Resnick, 1996; Corvo & Carpenter, 2000). Additionally, emerging evidence supports the existence of a correlation between caregiver substance abuse and children's exposure to violence (Ondersma, Delaney-Black, Covington, Nordstrom, & Sokol, 2006; Sprang, Clark, & Staton-Tindall, 2010). This analysis builds on prior research by examining the relationship between caregiver substance abuse and children's exposure to violence in a nationally representative sample of families investigated for child maltreatment.

Exposure to violence describes two types of experiences: direct victimization and witnessing violence (Finkelhor, Turner, Ormrod, & Hamby, 2009). Both types of exposure during childhood place children at greater risk for adverse proximal and distal outcomes related to traumatic stress. Children who directly experience violence through abuse or other situations have a greater likelihood of experiencing traumatic symptomology during childhood or adolescence (Boney-McCoy & Finkelhor, 1995; Fowler, Tompsett, Braciszewski, Jacques-Tiura, & Baltes, 2009). Experiencing abuse or violence in childhood might also increase the likelihood of subsequently experiencing posttraumatic stress disorder (PTSD) in adulthood (Brewin, Andrews, & Valentine, 2000; Hetzel & McCanne, 2005; Kulkarni, Graham-Bermann, Rauch, & Seng, 2011; Widom, 1999).

The relationship between witnessing violence as a child and subsequently experiencing PTSD is less straightforward (Feerick & Haugaard, 1999; Fowler et al., 2009; Kulkarni et al., 2011). The majority of the literature on children witnessing violence focuses on witnessing intimate partner violence (IPV). With child physical abuse estimated to co-occur in 45% to 70% of the families in which IPV is occurring, disentangling the relationship between direct victimization and witnessing violence and the impact each has on developing PTSD is complicated (Edleson, 1999; Holt, Buckley, & Whelan, 2008). Whereas Feerick and Haugaard (1999) found that women who witnessed IPV in childhood were more likely to report adult symptoms of PTSD even after controlling for childhood experiences of abuse, Kulkarni et al. (2011) found that witnessing domestic violence in childhood only predicted adult PTSD among women who also experienced childhood abuse.

However, a meta-analysis completed by Fowler et al. (2009) found that PTSD symptoms were equally predicted by experiencing violence, witnessing violence, or hearing about community violence. Although many studies focus on children witnessing IPV, emerging research reveals that witnessing community violence is also traumatic and harmful to child development. Findings from the Longitudinal Studies of Child Abuse and Neglect (LONGSCAN) demonstrated that a child's lifetime prevalence of exposure to community violence or IPV was associated with aggression, depression, and anxiety (Litrownik, Newton, Hunter, English, & Everson, 2003).

Although research indicates that exposure to violence might lead to negative consequences for children, it is still uncertain what impact caregiver substance abuse has on children's exposure to violence, particularly among child welfare samples. Preliminary studies indicate that children of substance-using caregivers might be at an increased risk for experiencing trauma. In a sample of 407 African American mothers and their 6- to 7-year-old children, caregiver alcohol abuse, the child's observation of drug use in the home, and the child's observation of drug deals were all significantly correlated with the child's exposure to violence (Ondersma et al., 2006). Reviewing a random sample of case records for 1,127 families with open child welfare cases in a Southern state, Sprang et al. (2010) found significant correlations between caregiver drug use (methamphetamine and other drugs) and the child's exposure to traumatic events. Sprang et al.'s results indicate that children of caregivers who use drugs, particularly those who use methamphetamines, are more likely to witness IPV, experience child endangerment, and experience child physical abuse than families with no record of substance use or misuse.

Prior research studies have examined caregiver substance abuse using data from the first National Survey of Child and Adolescent Well-Being (NSCAW I; Berger, Slack, Waldfogel, & Bruch, 2010; Carter, 2010; Phillips & Dettlaff, 2009; Phillips, Leathers, & Erkanli, 2009). Berger et al. (2010) examined the relationship between caseworker-identified substance abuse and case outcomes. The researchers found that cases with caseworker-identified substance abuse had poorer case outcomes, including higher levels of caseworker-reported risk and harm to the child and more frequent substantiation of child maltreatment and removal of the child from the home. Other studies have examined the role caregiver substance abuse plays in specific populations involved with CPS. Examining risk factors for the out-of-home placement of urban American Indian and Alaskan Native children, Carter (2010) found that urban American Indian and Alaskan Native children placed in out-of-home care were more likely to come from homes where caregiver substance abuse or mental health problems were present than White children. Prior research has also examined the prevalence of caregiver substance abuse among those who have previously been arrested and among caregivers on probation (Phillips & Dettlaff, 2009; Phillips et al., 2009). Due to the recent release of the National Survey of Child and Adolescent Well-Being II (NSCAW II) data, caregiver substance abuse and children's exposure to violence have not been explored in the NSCAW II beyond caregiver substance abuse prevalence rates reported in the baseline reports (Ringeisen, Casanueva, Smith, & Dolan, 2011). Using data from NSCAW II, this analysis examines the relationship between caregiver substance abuse and children's exposure to violence, both witnessing and experiencing, in a nationally representative sample of families involved with CPS.

The ecological-transactional model of child maltreatment (Cicchetti & Lynch, 1993; Cicchetti & Valentino, 2006) proposes that the child, the caregiver, and the environment have a reciprocal influence on each other that impacts child development and long-term outcomes. The theory proposes that potentiating and compensatory risk factors related to child maltreatment are present in each ecological system (macrosystem, exosystem, microsystem, and individual). These risk factors affect the transactions among the child, the family, and the environment. Using the ecological-transactional model of child maltreatment, it is proposed that caregiver substance abuse serves as a microsystem potentiating risk factor that has reciprocal interactions with the child's development, family interactions, and factors at the exosystem level. Furthermore, caregiver substance abuse could serve as an additional challenge in vulnerable child welfare families that tips the balance of the potentiating and compensatory factors, resulting in children experiencing negative outcomes like exposure to violence, as well as long-term consequences such as the development of PTSD. Based on this model, even among a sample of vulnerable children, many of whom have experienced maltreatment, the experience of violence exposure will further increase the likelihood of negative outcomes.

This study examines the correlation between caregiver substance abuse and children's exposure to violence in a nationally representative sample of families involved with CPS. This study tests the following hypotheses:

1. Among families involved with child welfare, children of substance-abusing caregivers will self-report higher rates of witnessing violence in the home than children of caregivers who are not abusing substances.
2. Among families involved with child welfare, children of substance-abusing caregivers will self-report higher rates of direct victimization in the home than children of caregivers who are not abusing substances.

METHODS

Data from the NSCAW II were analyzed to examine separately the relationships between alcohol use and child report of violence exposure and drug use and child report of violence exposure. The NSCAW II is the second in a series of national data collection studies of families investigated by CPS for child maltreatment. The total nationally representative sample consists of 5,872 children between the ages of 0 and 17.5 years and their families, who were investigated for child maltreatment between February 2008 and April 2009. Children were located in 81 primary sampling units (PSUs) nested within eight sampling strata at the state level. Seven of the eight strata are the states with the largest child welfare caseloads in the nation. The remaining stratum consists of all remaining states in the sample. A complex weighting strategy accounting for stratification, clustering, weighting, and oversampling of some subgroups was developed to make the PSUs nationally representative. Only one child per family was included in the NSCAW II. Therefore, children are not nested within caregivers. Additional information about the NSCAW II data set, study design, and data collection methods can be found elsewhere (see National Data Archive on Child Abuse and Neglect [NDACAN], 2010).

This secondary data analysis includes 1,652 children from the original sample of 5,872 who were at least 8 years of age at the time of the report. Age was used as an exclusion criterion because the Violence Exposure Scale for Children (VEX–R; Fox & Leavitt, 1995) was only administered to children 8 to 17 years of age. For this analysis, baseline data collected from caseworkers, the primary caregiver, and the child during in-person interviews were utilized. Caseworkers were interviewed at their agencies and were able to refer to their notes and case records during the interview.

Exposure to Violence

The dependent variable for this analysis, the child's self-report of witnessing or experiencing violence in the home, was measured with the VEX–R (Fox & Leavitt, 1995). The VEX–R measures children's exposure to violent and criminal acts in the home through the use of questions with cartoon illustrations. In the NSCAW II study, the cartoon illustrations and example questions (e.g., How many times have you watched TV?) were only used with children ages 8 to 10 (NDACAN, 2010). Children 11 to 18 were asked the questions that assess for violence exposure but they were not shown cartoon illustrations or asked the simple example questions to make the measure developmentally appropriate for older children.

To provide a sense of privacy to the children and increase the validity of the data, the VEX–R and other measures about sensitive topics were administered through Audio Computer-Assisted Self Interview (ACASI) for children 11 and older. Each child used headphones to listen to the audiotaped VEX–R questions and responded on a computer. Children 8 to 10 listened to the audiotaped VEX–R questions while wearing headphones and then pointed to their answers on cards held by the interviewer. Prior to starting the ACASI or audiotaped questions, the interviewer let each child know that the interviewer would not know his or her answers but responses indicating that the child's life or health was in danger would be reported to authorities to ensure the child's safety. Each child listened to sets of questions assessing whether or not he or she had witnessed or experienced the following acts committed by adults toward another person in a home in which they had lived: yelling, throwing something at, pushing or shoving hard, slapping hard, beating up, pointing a knife or gun, or the spanking of another child or themselves. Children were also asked if in a home in which they had lived they had witnessed but not experienced someone stealing from another person, stab another person with a knife, shoot another person with a gun, someone being arrested, or a person dealing drugs. Factor analyses of the VEX–R with groups of second and fourth graders indicate that questions on the measure group into two categories: mild violence and severe violence (Raviv et al., 2001). Severely violent behaviors included threatening with a knife or gun, stabbing, shooting, witnessing an arrest or drug deal, and stealing.

In a sample of minority preschoolers (Shahinfar, Fox, & Leavitt, 2000), the VEX–R was found to have moderate to good levels of interitem reliability for children's reports of exposure to violence (Cronbach's α = .80–.86). Internal consistency in the NSCAW sample is high for the total sample (Cronbach's $\alpha = .96$) and for the subscales (Cronbach's α = .86–.92; NDACAN, 2010). Shahinfar et al. (2000) found modest correlations between children's distress symptoms and scores on the VEX–R for witnessing mild violence ($r = .29$, $p < .05$), experiencing mild violence ($r = .22$, $p < .05$), and witnessing severe violence ($r = .25$, $p < .05$).

Substance Abuse

The independent variable of caregiver substance abuse was measured with caseworker responses to two separate questions on a risk assessment. Prior to administering the risk assessment questions, interviewers informed the caseworkers that they would be answering questions about the strengths and impairments of the caregivers. Caregiver alcohol abuse was dichotomized (yes or no) based on the CPS caseworker's response to the question, "At the time of the investigation, was there active alcohol abuse by [the primary caregiver]?" Caregiver drug abuse was dichotomized in the same manner based on the caseworker's response to the question, "At the time of the investigation, was there active drug abuse by [the primary caregiver]?" Primary caregivers were predetermined based on who was living in the home and providing care to the child. If the mother was one of these caregivers, she was considered the primary caregiver. This individual was identified by name in each of the preceding questions. Caseworkers were able to refer to all notes, documentation, and records for the case. Caseworkers were interviewed an average of 134 days after the investigation was completed (NDACAN, 2010). Caseworkers in the NSCAW II sample had an average of

7.1 years (median = 5.0) of experience working in the child welfare system (Dolan, Smith, Casanueva, & Ringeisen, 2011). Almost one quarter had a master's degree, 21.9% had a bachelor's degree in social work, and 52.3% had a bachelor's degree in a field other than social work (Dolan et al., 2011).

Control Variables

Child characteristics

The child characteristics of age, gender, and race or ethnicity were all controlled for in the analysis based on their significance in prior studies. Age was used as a continuous variable indicating the child's age in years. Prior examinations of the relationship between child age and exposure to violence indicate that age has a significant relationship with rates of exposure to violence but that the direction of this relationship has been inconsistent. Findings of some studies indicate older children report higher rates of exposure (Buka, Stichick, Birdthistle, & Earls, 2001; Richters & Martinez, 1993; Selner-O'Hagan, Kindlon, Buka, Raudenbush, & Earls, 1998), whereas others indicate that exposure to violence does not always have a positive linear relationship with age, as some younger children report higher rates of exposure (Schwab-Stone et al., 1995).

Child gender was a dichotomous categorical variable with children classified as either male or female. Although a number of studies indicate that male children are more likely to witness and experience violence than female children (Buka et al., 2001; Schwab-Stone et al., 1995; Selner-O'Hagan et al., 1998; Singer, Anglin, Song, & Lunghofer, 1995), a study by Attar, Guerra, and Tolan (1994) found that young elementary school girls reported higher rates of violence exposure than boys.

Child race or ethnicity was operationalized as a dichotomous categorical variable with non-Hispanic Caucasians being the comparison for all other races and ethnic groups. Race or ethnicity was also chosen as a control variable based on research indicating that ethnic minority children, both African American and Hispanics, are at higher risk for exposure to violence (Selner-O'Hagan et al., 1998; Singer et al., 1995).

Caregiver age

The caregiver characteristic of age was selected as a control variable. Caregiver age was used as a continuous variable indicating the caregiver's age in years at time of entry into the study.

Income

Household income was used as a control variable in the analysis based on its consistent association with children's exposure to violence. Household income was operationalized as primary caregiver report of the total household income combining all adult incomes. This variable was dichotomized into households with a combined annual income of $20,000 or more and households with a combined annual income of less than $20,000.

Data Analysis Strategy

Using logistic regression, baseline data from the NSCAW II were analyzed to examine separately the relationships between alcohol use and child report of violence exposure and drug use and child report of violence exposure. First, univariate analyses were conducted to determine sample characteristics. Next, chi-squares and *t* tests were conducted to examine the relationships between the exposure to violence variables and child age, child gender, child race or ethnicity, caregiver age, and household income. Chi-squares were also conducted to examine the relationship between the exposure to violence variables and caregiver alcohol and drug use. Finally, a total of eight separate logistic regression models were run for each of the four types of violence exposure (witnessing mild violence, witnessing severe violence, direct victimization with mild violence, direct victimization with severe violence) with each type of substance abuse (alcohol abuse and drug abuse). Data were analyzed in Stata/SE 12.1, and accounted for stratification, clustering, and weighting.

RESULTS

Sample Characteristics

In this sample (n = 1,652) of children 8 years and older, the mean age was slightly less than 12 years of age (M = 11.99, SD = 0.11) with a range of 8 to 17 years. There were fewer males in the sample than females (45.13% vs. 54.87%). Non-Hispanic Caucasian children made up 42.69% of the sample with 57.31% of the sample identifying as non-Hispanic African American, Hispanic, Asian, American Indian or Alaskan Native, or Native Hawaiian or Pacific Islander. Characteristics of the analyzed sample can be seen in Table 1.

Caregivers in the sample had a mean age of 38 years, 9.5 months (M = 38.76, SD = 0.35). Approximately half of the caregivers identified as non-Hispanic Caucasian (49.81%) with the other 50.19% identifying as non-Hispanic African American, Hispanic, Asian, American Indian or Alaskan Native, or Native Hawaiian or Pacific Islander. The mean annual household income for the sample was $27,877.00 ($SD$ = $1,533.21) with 50.58% of the sample having a household income greater than or equal to $20,000.

Caseworkers reported that 5.81% of the sample had an active drug abuse problem at the time of the investigation. This was higher than the 3.98% of

TABLE 1 Univariate Analyses

Variable	*M* or Percentage	*SD*
Child/caregiver variables		
Child age	11.99 years	.11
Child gender	45.13% male 54.87% female	
Child race	42.69% White 57.31% other	
Caregiver age	38.76 years	.35
Household income		
Continuous income	$27,877	$1,533.21
Dichotomous income	50.58% income $20,000+ 49.42% income less than $20,000	
Caseworker report of caregiver alcohol abuse	96.02% no 3.98% yes	
Caseworker report of caregiver drug abuse	94.19% no 5.81% yes	

TABLE 2 Child Self-Reported Exposure to Violence in the Home

Variable	Percentage
Witnessed mild violence	85.80% yes 14.20% no
Witnessed severe violence	54.73% yes 45.27% no
Victimized by mild violence	83.29% yes 16.71% no
Victimized by severe violence	5.21% yes 94.79% no
Any exposure to mild violence	90.59% yes 9.41% no
Any exposure to severe violence	54.78% yes 45.22% no
Any exposure to mild or severe violence	91.92% yes 8.08% no

the sample that caseworkers reported had an active alcohol abuse problem at the time of the investigation.

Violence Exposure

Results (see Table 2) indicate that 91.92% of all children in the sample had experienced some type of violence in the home either directly as a victim or indirectly as a witness.

Of the total sample, 90.59% had been exposed to one or more incidents of mild violence by witnessing, being victimized, or both. Of the total sample, 85.80% of children reported witnessing one or more incidents of mild violence and 83.29% reported experiencing one or more incidents of direct victimization with mild violence. Over half of the children in the total sample (54.78%) reported being exposed to one or more incidents of severe violence by witnessing, being victimized, or both. Over half of the total sample (54.73%) reported witnessing one or more incidents of severe violence and 5.21% of the total sample reported experiencing one or more incidents of direct victimization with severe violence.

Bivariate Analyses

The chi-square test indicated that active alcohol abuse by a caregiver is associated with the child witnessing mild violence, $\chi^2(1, n = 1210) = 18.49$, $p < .001$. A higher percentage of children of caregivers with active alcohol abuse (96.11%) reported witnessing mild violence in the home compared to children whose caregivers were not actively abusing alcohol (86.17%). A chi-square test indicated that active alcohol abuse by a caregiver is associated with the child witnessing severe violence, $\chi^2(1, n = 1208) = 58.00$, $p < .01$. A higher percentage of children of caregivers with active alcohol abuse (79.69%) reported witnessing severe violence in the home compared to children whose caregivers were not actively abusing alcohol (54.00%). However, chi-square tests indicated that there was no statistically significant association between active alcohol abuse by a caregiver and experiencing direct victimization with either mild violence or severe violence.

The chi-square test indicated that active drug abuse by a caregiver is associated with the child witnessing mild violence, $\chi^2(1, n = 1228) = 18.42$, $p < .05$. A higher percentage of children of caregivers with active drug abuse (94.46%) reported witnessing mild violence in the home compared to children whose caregivers were not actively abusing drugs (86.17%). A chi-square test indicated that active drug abuse by a caregiver is associated with the child witnessing severe violence, $\chi^2(1, n = 1225) = 56.50$, $p < .01$. A higher percentage of children of caregivers with active drug abuse (75.28%) reported witnessing severe violence in the home compared to children whose caregivers were not actively abusing drugs (53.98%). However, chi-square tests indicated that there was no statistically significant association between active drug abuse by a caregiver and experiencing direct victimization with either mild violence or severe violence.

There was a significant effect for child age on experiencing direct victimization by mild violence, $F(1, 72) = 5.98$, $p < .05$, with children who had been directly victimized by mild violence being older (M = 12.28 years, $SD = 0.11$) than children who had not (M = 11.66 years, SD = 0.25). However, there was no significant effect for child age on witnessing mild or severe violence or on experiencing direct victimization with severe violence.

Chi-square tests indicated that there was no statistically significant association between child gender and experiencing direct victimization or witnessing violence or between child race or ethnicity and experiencing direct victimization or witnessing violence.

There was a significant effect for caregiver age on witnessing severe violence, $F(1, 72) = 10.63$, $p < .01$, with children who had witnessed severe violence in the home having an older primary caregiver ($M = 39.83$, $SD = 0.46$) than children who had not ($M = 37.58$, $SD = 0.54$). No statistically significant differences in caregiver age were found for witnessing mild violence, experiencing direct victimization with mild violence, or experiencing direct victimization with severe violence.

There was a significant effect for household income on witnessing mild violence, $F(1, 72) = 21.14$, $p < .001$, with children who had witnessed mild violence in the home coming from homes with higher annual household incomes ($M = \$30,028.45$, $SD = \$1,852.29$) than children who had not witnessed mild violence in the home ($M = \$18,724.65$, $SD = \$1,565.14$). There was also a significant effect for household income on experiencing direct victimization with mild violence, $F(1, 72) = 12.16$, $p < .001$, with children who had experienced direct victimization with mild violence in the home again coming from homes with higher annual household incomes ($M = \$29,848.56$, $SD = \$1,913.24$) than children who had not experienced direct victimization with mild violence in the home ($M = \$21,384.40$, $SD = \$1,437.34$). No statistically significant differences in annual household income were found for witnessing severe violence or direct victimization with severe violence.

Regression Analyses

ALCOHOL ABUSE AND EXPOSURE TO VIOLENCE

The model regressing active alcohol abuse by a caregiver on children witnessing mild violence was statistically significant, $F(6, 67) = 4.23$, $p < .01$ (Table 3). Controlling for other variables in the model, the odds of a child of an alcohol-abusing caregiver witnessing mild violence are 3.22 times the odds of a child whose caregiver was not abusing alcohol ($t = 2.54$, $p < .05$). Controlling for other variables in the model, the odds of a child witnessing mild violence increased 2.1% for each \$1,000 increase in annual household income ($t = 4.13$, $p < .001$). Child age, child gender, child race, and caregiver age were not statistically significant in this model.

The model regressing active alcohol abuse by caregiver on children witnessing severe violence was statistically significant, $F(6, 67) = 3.97$, $p < .01$ (Table 3). Controlling for other variables in the model, the odds of a child of an alcohol-abusing caregiver witnessing severe violence are 3.22 times the odds of a child whose caregiver was not abusing alcohol ($t = 2.75$, $p < .01$). Controlling for other variables in the model, the odds of a child witnessing severe violence increased 2.9% for each 1-year increase in caregiver age ($t = 2.74$, $p < .01$). In this model, child age, child gender, child race, and household income were not statistically significant.

TABLE 3 Logistic Regression Results for Models Regressing Active Alcohol Abuse by Caregiver on Exposure to Violence

Model	Variable	*OR*	*SE*	*t*	*CI*	Model *F*
Active alcohol abuse on witnessing mild violence[a]						4.23**
	Active alcohol abuse	3.22	1.48	2.54*	[1.29, 8.07]	
	Child age	1.03	0.05	0.61	[0.93, 1.14]	
	Child gender	1.06	0.24	0.24	[0.67, 1.66]	
	Child race	0.61	0.20	−1.54	[0.32, 1.16]	
	Caregiver age	1.01	0.01	0.51	[0.98, 1.04]	
	Income	1.000021	$5.02*10^{-6}$	4.13***	[1.000011, 1.000031]	
Active alcohol abuse on witnessing severe violence[b]						3.97**
	Active alcohol abuse	3.22	1.37	2.75**	[1.38, 7.50]	
	Child age	1.04	0.04	0.93	[0.96, 1.11]	
	Child gender	0.72	0.13	−1.83	[0.50, 1.03]	
	Child race	1.12	0.20	0.64	[0.78, 1.61]	
	Caregiver age	1.03	0.01	2.74**	[1.01, 1.05]	
	Income	0.9999964	$2.89*10^{-6}$	−1.24	[0.9999906, 1.000002]	
Active alcohol abuse on mild violence victimization[c]						3.00*
	Active alcohol abuse	2.55	1.36	1.76	[0.89, 7.36]	
	Child age	1.05	0.05	0.92	[0.95, 1.16]	
	Child gender	0.81	0.18	−0.97	[0.52, 1.25]	
	Child race	0.77	0.20	−0.99	[0.45, 1.31]	
	Caregiver age	1.00	0.01	−0.30	[0.97, 1.02]	
	Income	1.000015	$4.61*10^{-6}$	3.33**	[1.000006, 1.000025]	
Active alcohol abuse on severe violence victimization[d]						1.79
	Active alcohol abuse	2.75	1.58	1.76	[0.88, 8.67]	
	Child age	1.01	0.13	0.10	[0.79, 1.30]	
	Child gender	0.53	0.24	−1.40	[0.22, 1.31]	
	Child race	0.43	0.23	−1.60	[0.15, 1.23]	
	Caregiver age	0.98	0.02	−1.02	[0.95, 1.02]	
	Income	1.000002	$4.89*10^{-6}$	0.34	[0.9999919, 1.000011]	

[a]$N = 1{,}160$. [b]$N = 1{,}158$. [c]$N = 1{,}159$. [d]$N = 1{,}146$.
*$p < .05$. **$p < .01$. ***$p < .001$.

The model regressing active alcohol abuse by a caregiver on children experiencing direct victimization with mild violence was also statistically significant, $F(6, 67) = 3.00$, $p < .05$. However, caregiver alcohol abuse was no longer statistically significant after controlling for the other variables in the model. The only statistically significant variable in the model was household income. After controlling for other variables in the model, the odds of a child experiencing direct victimization with mild violence increased 1.5% for each $1,000 increase in annual household income ($t = 3.33$, $p < .01$).

The model regressing active alcohol abuse by a caregiver on children experiencing direct victimization with severe violence was not statistically significant (Table 3).

DRUG ABUSE AND EXPOSURE TO VIOLENCE

The model regressing active drug abuse by caregiver on children witnessing mild violence was statistically significant, $F(6, 67) = 4.95$, $p < .001$ (Table 4). After controlling for other variables in the model, the odds of a child of a caregiver who was abusing drugs witnessing mild violence were 2.41 times

TABLE 4 Logistic Regression Results for Models Regressing Active Drug Abuse by Caregiver on Exposure to Violence

Model	Variable	*OR*	*SE*	*t*	*CI*	Model *F*
Active drug abuse on witnessing mild violence[a]						4.95***
	Active drug abuse	2.41	1.04	2.03*	[1.02, 5.71]	
	Child age	1.06	0.05	1.22	[0.96, 1.17]	
	Child gender	1.15	0.25	0.63	[0.74, 1.76]	
	Child race	0.66	0.21	−1.31	[0.36, 1.24]	
	Caregiver age	1.00	0.01	0.01	[0.97, 1.03]	
	Income	1.00002	$5.72*10^{-6}$	3.52**	[1.000009, 1.000032]	
Active drug abuse on witnessing severe violence[b]						3.73**
	Active drug abuse	2.39	0.81	2.56*	[1.21, 4.71]	
	Child age	1.05	0.04	1.37	[0.98, 1.12]	
	Child gender	0.73	0.13	−1.75	[0.51, 1.04]	
	Child race	1.16	0.20	0.86	[0.83, 1.62]	
	Caregiver age	1.03	0.01	2.74**	[1.01, 1.05]	
	Income	1.00	$2.90*10^{-6}$	−1.32	[0.9999904, 1.000002]	
Active drug abuse on mild violence victimization[c]						2.18
	Active drug abuse	1.11	0.38	0.30	[0.56, 2.19]	
	Child age	1.07	0.06	1.37	[0.97, 1.19]	
	Child gender	0.85	0.17	−0.77	[0.57, 1.28]	
	Child race	0.83	0.21	−0.74	[0.49, 1.39]	
	Caregiver age	0.99	0.01	−0.78	[0.97, 1.01]	
	Income	1.000015	$4.88*10^{-6}$	3.02**	[1.000005, 1.000024]	
Active drug abuse on severe violence victimization[d]						1.79
	Active drug abuse	0.81	0.51	−0.33	[0.23, 2.85]	
	Child age	1.02	0.13	0.18	[0.80, 1.31]	
	Child gender	0.51	0.23	−1.51	[0.21, 1.24]	
	Child race	0.39	0.21	−1.75	[0.14, 1.14]	
	Caregiver age	0.98	0.01	−1.10	[0.95, 1.01]	
	Income	1.000002	$5.17*10^{-6}$	0.33	[0.9999914, 1.000012]	

[a]$N = 1{,}173$. [b]$N = 1{,}170$. [c]$N = 1{,}172$. [d]$N = 1{,}157$.
*$p < .05$. **$p < .01$. ***$p < .001$.

the odds of a child whose caregiver was not abusing drugs ($t = 2.03$, $p < .05$). After controlling for other variables in the model, the odds of a child witnessing mild violence increased 2.0% for each $1,000 increase in annual household income ($t = 3.52$, $p < .01$). In this model, child age, child gender, child race, and caregiver age were not significant.

The model regressing active drug abuse by a caregiver on children witnessing severe violence was statistically significant, $F(6, 67) = 3.73$, $p < .01$. Controlling for other variables in the model, the odds of a child of caregiver who was abusing drugs witnessing severe violence are 2.39 times the odds of a child whose caregiver was not abusing drugs ($t = 2.56$, $p < .05$). Controlling for other variables in the model, the odds of a child witnessing severe violence increased 2.8% for each 1-year increase in caregiver age ($t = 2.74$, $p < .01$). In this model, child age, child gender, child race, and annual household income were not significant.

The model regressing active drug abuse by a caregiver on children experiencing direct victimization with mild violence and the model regressing active drug abuse by a caregiver on children experiencing direct victimization with severe violence were not statistically significant (Table 4).

DISCUSSION

Children involved with the child welfare system are reporting high levels of exposure to violence in the home. The results of this analysis indicate that the vast majority of children (91.92%) 8 and older who are involved with the child welfare system are reporting witnessing or experiencing at least one incident of violence in the home. Children reported high rates of both witnessing mild violence (85.80%) and experiencing victimization with mild violence (83.29%) in their homes. Of extreme concern, over half of the children in the sample (54.73%) reported witnessing at least one incident of severe violence in the home. These behaviors include witnessing an adult threaten another person with a knife or gun, witnessing a stabbing or shooting, witnessing an arrest or drug deal, and witnessing an adult steal from another person. Witnessing episodes of severe violence in childhood might increase the likelihood of experiencing PTSD in adulthood especially among a sample of children in which child maltreatment is prevalent (Feerick & Haugaard, 1999; Fowler et al., 2009; Kulkarni et al., 2011). Although only 5.21% of children 8 and older reported experiencing victimization in the home by severe violence, these children are highly likely to experience short- and long-term consequences due to this exposure (Boney-McCoy & Finkelhor, 1995; Brewin et al., 2000; Fowler et al., 2009; Hetzel & McCanne, 2005; Kulkarni et al., 2011; Widom, 1999). The prevalence of violence exposure among children in the child welfare system is concerning and likely contributes to the negative outcomes seen in this population.

Even among a population of vulnerable children at high risk for violence exposure, substance abuse by a caregiver was found to further increase the likelihood of witnessing both mild and severe violence in the home. Both alcohol abuse by a caregiver and drug abuse by a caregiver were associated with a higher likelihood of children witnessing mild and severe violence in the home. These findings were consistent in both bivariate and regression analyses. The hypothesis that among families involved with child welfare, children of caregivers who abuse substances will self-report higher rates of witnessing violence in the home than children of caregivers who are not abusing substances was supported. This finding is consistent with literature citing the high co-occurrence of IPV and substance abuse (Holt et al., 2008).

Results indicated that neither active alcohol abuse nor active drug abuse significantly increased the likelihood of child self-reports of experiencing mild or severe violence in the home. Therefore, the hypothesis that among families involved with child welfare, children of caregivers who abuse substances will self-report higher rates of direct victimization in the home than children of caregivers who are not abusing substances was rejected. Although prior studies have found a significant relationship between caregiver substance abuse and children experiencing violence (Sprang et al., 2010), caregiver substance abuse was not significantly related to higher rates of violent victimization among children 8 and older in the NSCAW II. This finding was consistent in both bivariate and logistic regression analyses. The sample of CPS-involved families in this study is unique from that of Sprang et al (2010). In the Sprang et al. study, all children (n = 1,127) were sampled from CPS records in the southern United States. The children were an average age of 5.1 years, predominantly White (71.3%), and the sample had slightly more males (52.6%) than females. Additionally, a large portion of the caregivers engaged in drug use in the Sprang et al. (2010) sample were using methamphetamines. With a mean age of 11.99 years, the sample of this study (n = 1,652) is older and has a higher percentage of females (54.87%) than those in the Sprang et al. study. The racially diverse sample has a lower percentage of White children (42.69%) than Sprang et al. Although both Sprang et al. (2010) and this study involve samples of CPS-involved families, the differences in sample characteristics might influence the relationship between caregiver substance abuse and children experiencing violence. Despite the finding that caregiver substance abuse did not significantly increase self-reported victimization rates in families with active caregiver substance abuse, it is important to recognize that children are reporting high levels of victimization in both families with and without caregiver substance abuse.

Although significant relationships between child gender and exposure to violence have been found in samples of urban elementary school-aged African American and Hispanic children (Attar et al., 1994), community samples of middle and high school students (Schwab-Stone et al., 1995; Singer et al., 1995), and children and young adults in Chicago (Selner-O'Hagan et al., 1998), this analysis did not find a statistically significant relationship between child gender and exposure to violence in a nationally representative sample of children 8 to 17 involved with the child welfare system. Prior studies have also found significant associations between child race or ethnicity and exposure to violence in community samples of high school students (Singer et al., 1995) and children and young adults in Chicago (Selner-O'Hagan et al., 1998). However, this analysis did not find a statistically significant relationship between child race or ethnicity and exposure to violence. The difference in findings might be due to differences between the community samples in prior studies and the CPS-involved families in this study. It is also possible that child gender and child race or ethnicity are associated with exposure to violence among certain subsamples of the child welfare population. The study completed by Attar et al. (1994) found that gender was associated with exposure to violence when interacting with ethnicity and when interacting with grade level. For example, first- and second-grade girls reported higher exposure to violence than fourth-grade boys but there were no significant differences with first- and second-grade boys or fourth-grade girls. Although no interactions were evident in this study, further analyses could examine the relationship between child gender and exposure to violence among subsets of the sample in this study.

Bivariate analyses found that children who reported experiencing direct victimization by mild violence were older ($M = 12.28$ years, $SD = 0.11$) than children who did not report ever experiencing this type of exposure to violence ($M = 11.66$ years, $SD = 0.25$). This finding is not surprising considering that children were asked if they have ever experienced this type of violence. Older children have had more time to acquire negative experiences. Interestingly, age was not found to differentiate children who had witnessed mild or severe violence or experienced severe violence. Future analyses should examine the number of reports of each type of violence exposure and its relationship with child age in the NSCAW II sample.

Bivariate and logistic regression analyses indicated a significant relationship between caregiver age and witnessing severe violence in the home. Children who reported witnessing severe violence in the home had older primary caregivers than children who did not witness severe violence in the home. Although rates of IPV have previously been found to be lower for older cohorts of women than younger cohorts of women (Rennison & Rand, 2003), the primary caregivers sampled in this study are relatively close in age ($M = 38.76$, $SD = 0.35$) and the caregiver age was examined continuously. Future analyses could further examine the relationship between caregiver age and children's exposure to violence in the NSCAW II data set by comparing a multinomial categorical variable of caregiver age to child's exposure to violence.

A surprising finding was the relationship between annual household income and children's exposure to violence. Results from bivariate analyses indicate children who reported witnessing mild violence or experiencing direct victimization with mild violence had higher annual household incomes than children who did not report these types of exposure to violence. Logistic regression analyses supported the relationship between higher income and witnessing mild violence in the home. This finding might reflect the generally low level of income for child welfare families ($M = \$27,877$, $SD = \$1,533.21$). Consistent with the ecological-transactional model of child maltreatment (Cicchetti & Lynch, 1993; Cicchetti & Valentino, 2006), families with higher incomes, which serve as a compensatory factor, might need to display much higher levels of distress and need to become involved in the CPS system. These findings indicating higher levels of exposure to mild violence in the home could be one potentiating factor initiating CPS involvement. Social workers should consistently assess for IPV among families involved with CPS regardless of household income.

Limitations

This analysis adds to the literature on the relationship between caregiver substance abuse and children experiencing direct victimization and witnessing violence in the home by examining these concepts in a nationally representative sample of child welfare families with children 8 to 17 years of age. However, it is limited by its inability to draw a conclusion on the relationship between caregiver substance abuse and children's exposure to community violence. As a secondary data analysis, the authors were limited to the data collected by the original research team. This analysis utilized caseworker reports of caregiver alcohol and drug use rather than caregiver self-reports. It is possible that caseworkers did not detect all active substance abuse by the primary caregivers. It is also possible that caseworkers reported active substance abuse for some caregivers who were not actively engaged in substance abuse. Although caregiver self-report is available for a sample of families in NSCAW II, caseworker report of alcohol and drug use was chosen for this analysis because it is available for families at all levels of CPS involvement, including families with children in the foster care system. Additionally, caseworkers were able to examine all case records when reporting whether or not the caregiver was involved in substance abuse. Although further detail is not available to examine how caseworkers determined that substance abuse was present, data available on the caseworkers indicates most were experienced child welfare professionals.

Although the VEX–R was developed to assess for exposure to violence in samples of children ages 4 to 10, the measure was administered to children 8 to 17 in NSCAW II. The illustrations and example questions were not used when children were over the age of 10. It is possible that the use of this measure in an older group of children could impact the validity of this measure. Children self-reported their exposure to violence. Even with the use of the ACASI technique, some children might have chosen to not report all episodes of witnessed or experienced violence. After being informed by the interviewer that responses indicating the child's health or safety were endangered would be reported to CPS, some children might have chosen not to report incidents that would meet these criteria.

Additionally, some critiques of the NSCAW II data include its use of eight strata with seven strata representing the states with the largest child welfare caseloads in the nation. The remaining stratum consists of all remaining states in the sample. Some researchers feel that the NSCAW II data set better represents the seven states with the largest child welfare caseloads in the country than it represents the remaining states. However, the intricate and complex use of weights is what makes the NSCAW II data set nationally representative (see NDACAN, 2010).

Implications

Implications for social work practice can be drawn from this analysis. First, when working with children from homes where active substance abuse by a caregiver is present or a history of substance abuse exists, social workers should gather information to assess the child's current exposure to violence and history of exposure to violence. Workers should assess for current or previous exposure to violence as both a direct victim and a witness. Second, when working with caregivers involved with CPS who are engaged in substance abuse, practitioners should be cognizant of the possibility of IPV in the home, assess for its presence and impact on children when safe to do so, and consider appropriate resources for the family. Third, when children report witnessing violence, experiencing victimization, or any trauma-related symptoms, interventions to address trauma symptoms must be utilized to prevent immediate and long-term negative outcomes.

CONCLUSION

This study adds to the literature by providing the first examination of the relationship between caregiver substance abuse and children's exposure to violence in a large, diverse, and nationally representative sample of families reported to CPS. This analysis, utilizing recently collected data, highlights the importance of assessing for exposure to violence among children involved with the child welfare system, particularly those where caregiver substance abuse is present. An additional wave of data is currently being collected for the NSCAW II study. In addition to the future directions already discussed, future research should examine the relationship between caregiver substance abuse and exposure to violence over time.

REFERENCES

Attar, B. K., Guerra, N. G., & Tolan, P. H. (1994). Neighborhood disadvantage, stressful life events, and adjustment in urban elementary-school children. *Journal of Clinical Child Psychology, 23*, 391–400.

Berger, L. M., Slack, K. S., Waldfogel, J., & Bruch, S. K. (2010). Caseworker-perceived caregiver substance abuse and child protective services outcomes. *Child Maltreatment, 15*(3), 199–201. doi:10.1177/1077559510368305

Besinger, B. A., Garland, A. F., Litrownik, A. J., & Landsverk, J. A. (1999). Caregiver substance abuse among maltreated children placed in out-of-home care. *Child Welfare, 78*(2), 221–239.

Boney-McCoy, S., & Finkelhor, D. (1995). Psychosocial sequelae of violent victimization in a national youth sample. *Journal of Consulting and Clinical Psychology, 63*(5), 726–736.

Brewin, C. R., Andrews, B., & Valentine, J. D. (2000). Meta-analysis of risk factors for posttraumatic stress disorder in trauma-exposed adults. *Journal of Consulting and Clinical Psychology, 68*(5), 748–766. doi:10.1037//0022-006X.68.5.748

Buka, S. L., Stichick, T. L., Birdthistle, I., & Earls, F. J. (2001). Youth exposure to violence: Prevalence, risks, and consequences. *American Journal of Orthopsychiatry, 71*(3), 298–310.

Carter, V. B. (2010). Factors predicting placement of urban American Indian/Alaska Natives into out-of-home care. *Children and Youth Services Review, 32*(5), 657–663. doi:10.1016/j.childyouth.2009.12.013

Chandy, J. M., Blum, R. W., & Resnick, M. D. (1996). History of sexual abuse and parental alcohol misuse: Risk, outcomes and protective factors in adolescents. *Child & Adolescent Social Work Journal, 13*(5), 411–432.

Cicchetti, D., & Lynch, M. (1993). Toward an ecological/transactional model of community violence and child maltreatment: Consequences for children's development. *Psychiatry, 56*, 96–118.

Cicchetti, D., & Valentino, K. (2006). An ecological-transactional perspective on child maltreatment: Failure of the average expectable environment and its influence on child development. In D. Cicchetti & D. Cohen (Eds.), *Developmental psychopathology* (2nd ed., pp. 129–201). Hoboken, NJ: Wiley.

Corvo, K., & Carpenter, E. H. (2000). Effects of parental substance abuse on current levels of domestic violence: A possible elaboration of intergenerational transmission processes. *Journal of Family Violence, 15*(2), 123–135.

Dolan, M., Smith, K., Casanueva, C., & Ringeisen, H. (2011). *NSCAW II baseline report: Caseworker characteristics, child welfare services, and experiences of children placed in out-of-home care* (OPRE Rep. No. 2011-27e). Washington, DC: Office of Planning, Research and Evaluation, Administration for Children and Families, U.S. Department of Health and Human Services.

Edleson, J. L. (1999). Introduction to special issue. *Child Maltreatment, 4*(2), 91–92.

Feerick, M. M., & Haugaard, J. J. (1999). Long-term effects of witnessing marital violence for women: The contribution of childhood physical and sexual abuse. *Journal of Family Violence, 14*(4), 377–398.

Finkelhor, D., Turner, H., Ormrod, R., & Hamby, S. L. (2009). Violence, abuse, and crime exposure in a national sample of children and youth. *Pediatrics, 124*, 1411–1423. doi:10.1542/peds.2009-0467

Fowler, P. J., Tompsett, C. J., Braciszewski, J. M., Jacques-Tiura, A. J., & Baltes, B. B. (2009). Community violence: A meta-analysis on the effect of exposure and mental health outcomes of children and adolescents. *Development and Psychopathology, 21*, 227–259. doi:10.1017/S0954579409000145

Fox, N. A., & Leavitt, L. A. (1995). *The violence exposure scale for children (VEX–R)*. College Park, MD: University of Maryland.

Hetzel, M. D., & McCanne, T. R. (2005). The roles of peritraumatic dissociation, child physical abuse, and child sexual abuse in the development of posttraumatic stress disorder and adult victimization. *Child Abuse and Neglect, 29*, 915–930. doi:10.1016/j.chiabu.2004.11.008

Holt, S., Buckley, H., & Whelan, S. (2008). The impact of exposure to domestic violence on children and young people: A review of the literature. *Child Abuse & Neglect, 32*, 797–810. doi:10.1016/j.chiabu.2008.02.004

Jones, L. (2004). The prevalence and characteristics of substance abusers in a child protective service sample. *Journal of Social Work Practice in the Addictions, 4*(2), 33–50. doi:10.1300/J160v04n02_04

Kulkarni, M. R., Graham-Bermann, S., Rauch, S. A. M., & Seng, J. (2011). Witnessing versus experiencing direct violence in childhood as correlates of adulthood PTSD. *Journal of Interpersonal Violence, 26*(6), 1264–1281. doi:10.1177/0886260510368159

Litrownik, A. J., Newton, R., Hunter, W. M., English, D., & Everson, M. D. (2003). Exposure to family violence in young at-risk children: A longitudinal look at the effects of victimization and witnessed physical and psychological aggression. *Journal of Family Violence, 18*(1), 59–73.

National Data Archive on Child Abuse and Neglect. (2010). *National Survey of Child and Adolescent Well-Being (NSCAW): NSCAW II, Wave 1 data files user's manual restricted release version*. Ithaca, NY: Author.

Ondersma, S. J., Delaney-Black, V., Covington, C. Y., Nordstrom, B., & Sokol, R. J. (2006). The association between caregiver substance abuse and self-reported violence exposure among young urban children. *Journal of Traumatic Stress, 19*(1), 107–118.

Phillips, S. D., & Dettlaff, A. J. (2009). More than parents in prison: The broader overlap between the criminal justice and child welfare systems. *Journal of Public Child Welfare, 3*(1), 3–22. doi:10.1080/15548730802690718

Phillips, S. D., Leathers, S. J., & Erkanli, A. (2009). Children of probationers in the child welfare system and their families. *Journal of Child and Family Studies, 18*(2), 183–191. doi:10.1007/s10826-008-9218-x

Raviv, A., Erel, O., Fox, N. A., Leavitt, L. A., Raviv, A., Dar, I., . . . Greenbaum, C. W. (2001). Individual measurement of exposure to everyday violence among elementary schoolchildren across various settings. *Journal of Community Psychology, 29*(2), 117–140.

Rennison, C., & Rand, M. R. (2003). Nonlethal intimate partner violence against women: A comparison of three age cohorts. *Violence Against Women, 9*(12), 1417–1428. doi:10.1177/1077801203259232

Richters, J. E., & Martinez, P. (1993). The NIMH community violence project: I. Children as victims of and witnesses to violence. *Psychiatry, 56*, 7–21.

Ringeisen, H., Casanueva, C., Smith, K., & Dolan, M. (2011). *NSCAW II baseline report: Caregiver health and services* (OPRE Rep. No. 2011-27d). Washington,

DC: Office of Planning, Research and Evaluation, Administration for Children and Families, U.S. Department of Health and Human Services.

Schwab-Stone, M. E., Ayers, T. S., Kasprow, W., Voyce, C., Barone, C., Shriver, T., & Weissberg, R. P. (1995). No safe haven: A study of violence exposure in an urban community. *Journal of the American Academy of Child and Adolescent Psychiatry, 34*(10), 1343–1352.

Selner-O'Hagan, M. B., Kindlon, D. J., Buka, S. L., Raudenbush, S. W., & Earls, F. J. (1998). Assessing exposure to violence in urban youth. *The Journal of Child Psychology and Psychiatry, 39*(2), 215–224.

Shahinfar, A., Fox, N. A., & Leavitt, L. A. (2000). Preschool children's exposure to violence: Relation of behavior problems to parent and child reports. *American Journal of Orthopsychiatry, 70*, 115–125.

Singer, M. I., Anglin, T. M., Song, L. Y., & Lunghofer, L. (1995). Adolescents' exposure to violence and associated symptoms of psychological trauma. *The Journal of the American Medical Association, 273*(6), 477–482.

Sprang, G., Clark, J. J., & Staton-Tindall, M. (2010). Caregiver substance use and trauma exposure in young children. *Families in Society, 91*(4), 401–407. doi:10.1606/1044-3894.4029

U.S. Department of Health and Human Services, Administration for Children and Families, Administration on Children, Youth and Families, Children's Bureau. (2011). *Child maltreatment 2010*. Retrieved from http://www.acf.hhs.gov/programs/cb/stats_research/index.htm#can

U.S. Government Accounting Office. (1994). *Foster care: Parental drug abuse has alarming impact on young children* (Rep. No. GAO/HEHS-94-89). Washington, DC: Author.

U.S. Government Accounting Office. (1998). *Foster care: Agencies face challenges securing stable homes for children of substance abusers* (Rep. No. GAO/HEHS-98-182). Washington, DC: Author.

Widom, C. S. (1999). Posttraumatic stress disorder in abused and neglected children grown up. *American Journal of Psychiatry, 156*(8), 1223–1229.

Advancing Trauma-Informed Systems Change in a Family Drug Treatment Court Context

LAURIE A. DRABBLE, PhD, MSW, MPH
Professor, School of Social Work, San Jose State University, San Jose, California, USA

SHELBY JONES, MSW
Graduate Research Assistant, School of Social Work, San Jose State University, San Jose, California, USA

VIVIAN BROWN, PhD
Founder and Former CEO, PROTOTYPES Centers for Innovation in Health, Mental Health and Social Services, Manhattan Beach, California, USA

A growing body of literature documents the importance of trauma-informed and trauma-specific services and systems change in both addiction treatment and child welfare fields. The overall aim of this qualitative study was to explore barriers, benefits, and facilitating factors associated with a trauma-informed systems assessment and improvement initiative conducted in the context of a family drug treatment court (FDTC). Semistructured in-depth interviews with 12 key informants and historical analyses of project documents over a 4-year time span were conducted. Results underscore the relevance of trauma-informed systems change in collaborative contexts designed to address the complex needs of children and families.

Planning for this research was supported in part by the Institute for Collaborative Response for Victims of Family Violence, San Jose State University.

A growing body of literature documents the importance of addressing trauma in both addiction treatment and child welfare (Hodas, 2006; Ko et al., 2008; McHugo, Caspi, et al., 2005; National Association of State Mental Health Program Directors and National Technical Assistance Center for State Mental Health Planning, 2004; Savage, Quiros, Dodd, & Bonavota, 2007). There is also considerable agreement about the need for addiction treatment, child welfare, and dependency court systems to work collaboratively (Carlson, 2006; Drabble, 2011; Green, Rockhill, & Burrus, 2008; Marsh, Smith, & Bruni, 2010; U.S. Department of Health and Human Services [DHHS], 1999; Young, Boles, & Otero, 2007). Collaborative models of practice, such as family drug treatment courts (FDTCs), appear to be promising in terms of positive outcomes for both parental treatment participation and parent–child reunification (Boles, Young, Moore, & DiPirro-Beard, 2007; Carlson, 2006; Green, Furrer, Worcel, Burrus, & Finigan, 2007; Osterling & Austin, 2008; Ryan, Marsh, Testa, & Louderman, 2006; Worcel, Furrer, Green, Burrus, & Finigan, 2008). However, there is a paucity of literature examining how trauma-informed systems changes might be advanced in a collaborative context, such as FDTCs.

IMPORTANCE OF ADDRESSING TRAUMA

Research indicates that trauma is a defining, reoccurring event in the lives of individuals with both substance abuse and mental health disorders (Bryer, Nelson, Miller, & Krol, 1987; Kilpatrick, Acierno, Resnick, Saunders, & Best, 1997; Najavits, Weiss, & Shaw, 1997). For example, one of the largest, most representative studies examining the long-term effects of trauma, the Adverse Childhood Experiences (ACE) study of more than 17,000 women and men, found strong correlations between childhood trauma and long-term negative health outcomes, including addiction (Dube, Felitti, Dong, Giles, & Anda, 2003; Felitti et al., 1998). Although treatment services and systems have often neglected to address trauma in the lives of adults with co-occurring disorders (Becker et al., 2005; Timko & Moos, 2002), an emerging body of literature documents the value of integrating a trauma lens in addiction treatment and mental health services. For example, the Women, Co-Occurring Disorders and Violence Study (WCDVS), a quasi-experimental, nine-site, longitudinal study, examined the prevalence of trauma among more than 2,000 women with co-occurring disorders, as well as outcomes when treatment was integrated (McHugo, Kammerer, et al., 2005). Results from the WCDVS found the trauma-informed framework to be a helpful paradigm, not only for understanding the complex issues facing women with co-occurring disorders, but also for improving outcomes (Amaro, Chernoff, Brown, Arévalo, & Gatz, 2007; Becker et al., 2005; McHugo, Caspi, et al., 2005; McHugo, Kammerer, et al., 2005; Morrissey, Ellis, et al., 2005; Morrissey, Jackson, et al., 2005; Reed & Mazelis, 2005; Savage et al., 2007). Although many of the consumers in the WCDVS study were involved in child welfare systems, extension of trauma-informed services and systems change into dependency court contexts were not explored in this body of research.

Research also documents the importance of addressing trauma in childhood, including incorporating the family in treatment (Hodas, 2006; Ko et al., 2008). "Trauma informed care must begin with the provision of safety, both physical and emotional, by adult caregivers to the traumatized child" (Hodas, 2006, p. 32). In addition, research indicates that "families in particular remain the single most important resource for a child dealing with trauma exposure and trauma-related symptoms" (Hodas, 2006, p. 48). Addressing child maltreatment in collaboration with parents through a trauma-informed, strengths-based lens has the potential to reduce future instances of child trauma and keep families together. National studies document that risk factors for child maltreatment are caregiver substance abuse, caregiver exposure to domestic violence, and caregiver mental health (National Center for Injury Prevention and Control, 2005a, 2005b). The prevalence of trauma among caregivers with these co-occurring problems indicates that trauma-informed care and systems change is not only important for children's services, but also for services working with parents, such as FDTCs.

TRAUMA-INFORMED SYSTEMS

In a trauma-informed system, trauma is not only recognized as an event or series of events in an individual's life span, but as a life-altering experience that can form the "core" of an individual's identity (Harris & Fallot, 2001). A trauma-informed system is one that "incorporates knowledge about trauma" in every area of its service delivery system, both within an individual system and across systems (Harris & Fallot, 2001). Developing trauma-informed systems is not easy, as it involves a vital cultural shift. According to Harris and Fallot (2001), a trauma-informed system must incorporate principles of safety, trustworthiness, choice, collaboration, and empowerment at every level.

Trauma-informed systems are characterized by principles of client choice, empowerment, collaboration, safety and respect, resilience, and the goal to minimize organizational retraumatization (Elliott, Bjelajac, Fallot, Markoff, & Reed, 2005). In addition, Harris and Fallot (2001) argued that a trauma-informed system must understand not only the trauma history of their clients, but also the larger societal factors contributing to violence and victimization that are common among consumers of mental health and substance abuse services. A trauma-informed system must then use this knowledge to inform the design of the system, including how the system accommodates the vulnerabilities of trauma survivors as well as how the system incorporates client choice in treatment (Harris & Fallot, 2001).

Implementation science provides a framework for considering how organizations and systems engage in a strategic effort to mainstream innovations based on new knowledge and research findings through four essential activities: planning, engaging, executing, and evaluating (Mildon & Shlonsky, 2011). Mildon and Shlonsky (2011) argued that passive uptake strategies are insufficient, as they fail to adequately engage practitioners or address contextual challenges to implementation. There are many strategies involved in becoming a trauma-informed system, which are consistent with implementation science. Specific strategies include administrative commitment to change, universal screening for trauma histories among clients, training and education on trauma, hiring practices, and a holistic review of policies and procedures (Harris & Fallot, 2001). Implementation of organizational and systems change requires consideration of contextual issues, including barriers to change. Some researchers have associated the barriers to recovery from trauma to "organizational stress," or "collective systemic trauma" (Bloom, 2006, p. 25). In some cases, power differentials involved in different systems, such as that between a client and a social worker or judge, can replicate the dynamics of power and control involved in family and community violence. Bloom (2006) stated, "Recovery begins with safety, and without addressing organizational change we fear the recovery movement will not have the impact it must have for true transformational change" (p. 25).

Historically, systems serving individuals with co-occurring disorders (e.g., trauma, mental health issues, health problems, and substance use disorders) have been characterized by compartmentalization, fragmentation, and a tendency for systems to operate independently from one another (Harris & Fallot, 2001). Successful collaboration among addiction treatment, child welfare, and dependency courts requires development and articulation of shared values; adoption of specific evidence-based practices for children and families; implementation of collaborative systems changes (e.g., training, budgeting, and information sharing), and development of shared outcomes (Young & Gardner, 2002). These dimensions of collaboration are relevant to the integration of trauma-informed systems change in the context of research, which continues to document the importance of trauma as a pivotal connection between service delivery systems and focal point for evidence-based, consumer-centered practice (British Columbia Center of Excellence for Women's Health, 2011).

TRAUMA AND THE COURTS

FDTCs are specialized courts that operate under the juvenile dependency court system. "These courts provide the setting for a collaborative effort by the court and all the participants in the child protection system to come together in a non-adversarial setting to determine the individual treatment needs of substance-abusing parents whose children are under the jurisdiction of the dependency court" (Edwards & Ray, 2005, p. 1). FDTC settings provide frequent court hearings and support from a team of representatives from the court, child welfare, substance abuse treatment, and other service providers (Green et al., 2007). FDTC models appear to be associated with greater success in treatment and higher reunification rates compared to clients who receive traditional child welfare services (Green et al., 2007; Worcel et al., 2008).

Perhaps some of the most adversarial systems that trauma survivors might experience are the courts. However, few studies examine explicitly the prevalence and dynamics of trauma in court settings, including collaborative court settings, such as FDTC that are intended to minimize adversarial dynamics. One notable exception to the dearth of research on this topic is a study by Lesperance et al. (2001), which found participants in FDTC (N = 25) reported similar experiences of trauma as that of women in the WCDVS, with a reported average lifetime exposure to 12 stressful events, lifetime frequency of 12 different events of interpersonal abuse, and an average frequency of two incidences of childhood physical or sexual abuse. Trauma was also linked to risky behaviors in substance-abusing parents (Lesperance et al., 2001). Similarly, among court-referred youth in the juvenile justice system, studies have found the prevalence of trauma and posttraumatic stress disorder to be up to 75% for females and 51.3% for males (Brosky & Lally, 2004). Researchers have recognized the prevalence of family violence among youth and emphasize the importance of strategies to make the court process less adversarial and more supportive of recovery (Buel, 2003; Worcel et al., 2008).

Access to timely substance abuse treatment and efforts to maximize success in treatment for substance use disorders are important to reunification and permanency for children in the child welfare system (DHHS, 1999). Stringent timelines for reunification mandated by the Adoption and Safe Families Act amplify pressures for courts and partnered service delivery systems to optimize opportunities for successful recovery (DHHS Administration for Children and Families, 1997; Green, Rockhill, & Furrer, 2006). Despite the prevalence of trauma among clients and the urgency for timely access to effective treatment, few studies examine potential retraumatization of these clients as a result of participation in the court process, and even fewer studies have examined what helps and hinders trauma-informed systems change in court contexts.

The overall aim of this study was to examine the process and outcomes of a trauma-informed system assessment conducted within an FDTC. Specific research questions include the following:

1. What were the core strategies associated with the implementation of a trauma-informed assessment process?
2. What were the benefits, barriers, and facilitating factors related to trauma-informed systems change?

METHODS

This qualitative study used a combination of semistructured, in-depth interviews with 12 key informants and historical analysis of project documents over a 4-year time span. The site of study was one cross-system, collaborative FDTC located in a diverse California county, with a population of almost 2 million individuals, of whom 58% were Caucasian, 33% were Asian American, and 27% were Hispanic. The project is a collaborative FDTC within the child dependency court system that specifically serves parents with alcohol and other drug use disorders who have children under the age of three. The project was one of 53 sites funded to improve outcomes for children impacted by parental substance abuse (see DHHS, 2010). The goals of the FDTC include early identification of treatment issues, rapid engagement and retention in treatment, and comprehensive, collaborative response from service providers. This study was conducted in collaboration with the FDTC and implemented by a volunteer research team of faculty and graduate students from a local university.

Sample

Purposive sampling was employed to recruit interviewees representing the FDTC and partner systems, who were closely involved in collaborative planning and project implementation over the course of the first 4 years of the project. Key informants were selected from a pool of approximately 40 professionals who were involved in FDTC strategic planning or direct implementation based on the following criteria: (a) involvement in FDTC, (b) inclusion of individuals from different systems, and (c) knowledge of trauma-informed systems change efforts in FDTC. The final sample included 12 key informants over the age of 18, representing the court and legal services (n = 3), peer mentor (n = 1), drug and alcohol treatment (n = 2), child welfare and children's services (n = 3), mental health (n = 1), domestic violence services (n = 1), and trauma consultants (n = 1).

Interview Guide and Data Collection Procedures

Interviews were conducted using a semistructured interview guide, took approximately 45 to 60 minutes, and were audiotaped with the permission of the interviewee. The interview guide was designed to explore research questions based on seven open-ended questions and follow-up probe questions in three broad areas: (a) reflection about the process of, and insights derived from, conducting trauma-informed systems assessments; (b) benefits and barriers related to trauma-informed systems change efforts; and (c) impact and "lessons learned" from participating in trauma-informed systems change efforts. Interviews took place between December 2011 and February

2012. Historical data included biannual reports and documents summarizing results of trauma-informed systems assessments. In-depth interviews were transcribed verbatim.

ANALYSIS

Content analysis of interview transcripts was conducted to identify common themes related to facilitating factors, barriers, and benefits to implementing trauma-informed systems changes. Two authors read a sample of transcripts from respondents representing different systems and independently developed a list of provisional codes, which were reviewed and refined for use as a start list of codes. Initial open coding to conceptualize, compare, and categorize data was followed by an iterative process to further define and identify connections between categories in the data (Strauss, 1987; Strauss & Corbin, 1990). New codes were developed and existing codes were rearranged or modified throughout the first phase of analysis. Researchers (the first and second authors) used a consensus model in reviewing, revising, and finalizing themes to strengthen trustworthiness of the analysis. The third author was consulted as needed in resolving discrepancies or questions that arose in the analysis process.

Secondary data from project documents and trauma-informed systems assessments previously conducted at FDTC were also analyzed. Historical data included summary documents and attachments from seven semiannual reports, strategic planning session summaries, and findings of a special FDTC trauma assessment. Data for the semiannual and special reports were compiled primarily by project staff and consultants, with input and oversight from leaders in partner systems. Data from these documents were analyzed for themes pertaining to core strategies for trauma-informed system improvements and findings of trauma-informed system assessment. Data from historical documents were triangulated with data from narrative interviews to reduce potential bias and to address potential gaps in the narrative data from in-depth interviews. Preliminary findings were reviewed during a meeting of FDTC system leaders, many of whom were interviewed for the study, to verify the trustworthiness of the findings.

RESULTS

Core Strategies for Advancing Trauma-Informed Systems Change

The FDTC identified trauma-informed systems change as a pivotal goal and use of a trauma-informed perspective as a core value during the formative months of the project (in 2008). Review of historical FDTC documents, as well as responses from key informants, revealed several intersecting strategies for advancing trauma-informed systems changes during the formation and implementation of the project. The prevalence of trauma among program participants was discussed, and the need for trauma-informed systems change was prioritized early in the project by a strategic planning team that included more than 30 leaders and providers across systems (courts, children's services, mental health, addiction treatment, attorneys, representatives of a mentor parent project, domestic violence service providers, and other partners). Based on interviews and a review of historical documents, this section highlights key strategies and activities that were initiated during the strategic planning process and implemented over the formative years of the project.

One of the pivotal components of the overall strategy involved conducting trauma-informed "walk-through" assessments adapted by Dr. Vivian Brown (based on the work of Fallot & Harris, 2006) as a tool for helping agencies and systems recognize potential trauma triggers within their agency and develop mitigation strategies for addressing change. The assessment includes questions such as whether the facility or system offers a safe place for clients and families; whether screening includes substance use, mental health, and trauma questions; the degree to which clients receive clear explanations and information about program procedures; types of choices clients are given about services; and sensitivity of staff to the potential of retraumatization during certain procedures. In addition to these questions, the trauma assessment walk-through includes questions related to the system's current status and readiness for change, including administrative support for trauma-informed services and opportunities for trauma training. Review of historical documents as well as responses from interviewees regarding their experience of the trauma-informed walk-throughs revealed the assessment's strengths, limitations, and potential for furthering trauma-informed systems change efforts in the courts and partner systems. Some of the potential strategies that were identified from the trauma assessments and recorded in the historical documents included the development of a specialized trauma-informed parenting module, training on trauma and men, training for court staff, and development of trauma-informed child activities. All of these were subsequently developed and implemented.

IDENTIFICATION OF TRAUMA TRIGGERS AND ACTION STEPS

Interviewees who had participated in the assessment process uniformly described the process as effective in surfacing specific potential trauma triggers and generating ideas for reducing or eliminating triggers. "What everyone was asked to do was basically put themselves in the shoes of a client," noted one participant. One respondent stated, "The training enhanced having an 'eye' towards a trauma-informed facility." Other informants commented, "We had good cross-participation and great potential action steps came out of it." "We were sobered by the process and then sobered by some of the challenges." "Just the concept of doing a trauma-informed survey reframes everything. It heightens the awareness of what our parents have to go through, and what their kids have to go through." Examples of triggers described by interviewees and documented in historical documents included crowded waiting rooms that were stressful for children, presence of security personnel, and intimidating court processes and environment. Illustrations of specific strategies for mitigating some of these potential triggers included creation of a space designed for children in the waiting area, provision of training for security personnel about trauma and trauma reactions, and improved preparation for parents about what to expect in court.

Exploration of options for change in systems and among providers

Many respondents commented on the "feedback" of the trauma consultant as being particularly helpful throughout the walk-through. Ideas generated in discussion with the consultant and other participants "made sense to the team." The exploration also challenged individuals to examine how they might inadvertently contribute to retraumatizing clients. One participant observed, "It was helpful to kind of check in with [the consultant] to see, for me, at least my role, how I'm communicating with clients, whether, you know, if it's appropriate? Could that be more traumatic, the way that I communicate?"

Flexibility in method of assessment (in-person vs. via telephone)

The assessment was designed to be flexible for use in various settings, and conducted with a small team (of two to four) individuals. Agencies that participate in the assessment generally did so by having the team members physically walk through their agency while considering various practices and procedures. To accommodate schedules of multiple court partners, a virtual walk-through was conducted over several telephone meetings with a larger group (8–10 participants). Interviewees who participated in telephone assessment meetings noted that the process was both productive and increased opportunities for participation. Others commented on the challenge of conducting the walk-through over the phone, noting "It was a little constraining . . . when someone is on the speaker box, it's harder not to talk over somebody else." However, limitations that were raised did not overshadow the value of the walk-throughs and the important trauma-related issues that were raised and addressed as a result of the assessment.

Parallel processes across partner systems

FDTC historical documents and interviews revealed that the trauma-informed systems assessment served as a strong catalyst for new trauma-informed change initiatives in several partner systems. The assessment process also augmented the work of partner systems that had already initiated similar processes to implement trauma-informed services and systems change within their own agencies. These parallel processes were noted as a positive outcome of the trauma-informed initiative of FDTC.

Training with experts in trauma-informed interventions and systems

Historical documents and interviews also reflected the value of trauma-related training designed to support trauma-informed systems changes. Trainings were provided on multiple levels: training with direct FDTC providers and court staff, training for all partner systems through interdisciplinary conferences and training, and targeted training for partners on key and emerging topics of interest (e.g., trigger identification and deescalation strategies, men and trauma, child-specific trauma activities). Partner agencies implemented additional trainings, frequently providing for participation of staff from other service delivery systems. Although interviewees (and historical documents) generally described this constellation of assessment and training activities as strengths, several also highlighted the need for more effective communication and collaboration across systems to maximize benefits across agencies.

Benefits, Barriers, and Facilitating Factors in Trauma-Informed Systems Change

The benefits, as well as key barriers and facilitating factors in advancing trauma informed systems change, are summarized in Figure 1. Themes in these three overarching areas were derived primarily from in-depth interviews.

Benefits of trauma-informed systems change

Interview responses regarding the benefits of implementing trauma-informed systems change were described as resulting in (a) increased awareness of trauma, (b) benefits for the clients, and (c) benefits for service providers and systems.

Increased awareness of trauma through adoption of a "trauma lens." Interviewees generally felt positive about the process of undergoing trauma-informed systems change and felt it was helpful in understanding their clients, their histories, and the effects of trauma on their ability to parent and connect with their children. One response typified interviewee comments: "One of the really great things that has come out of this whole process is a much higher level of awareness of trauma and providing trauma-informed,

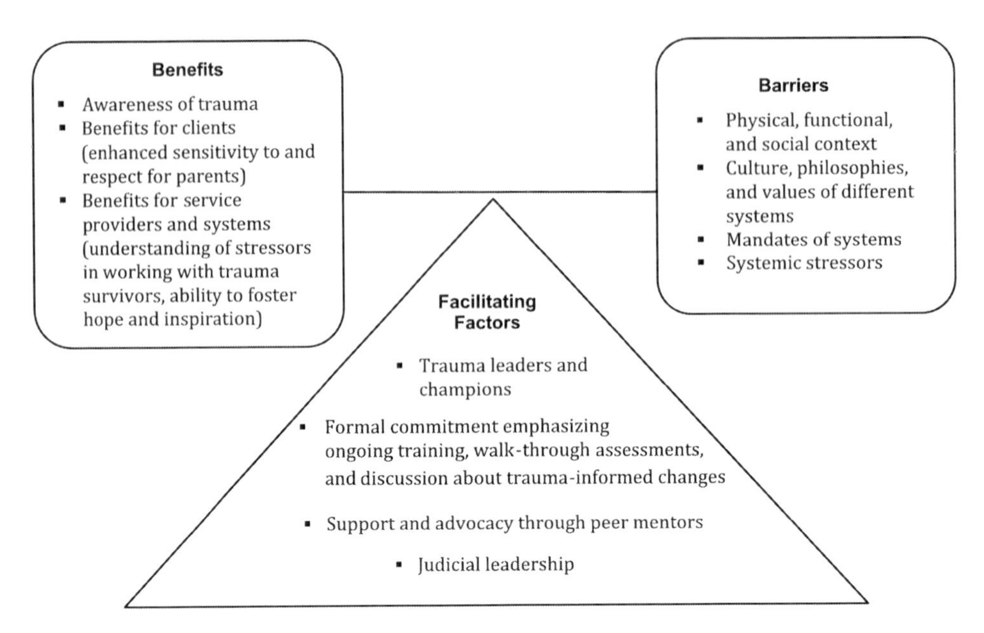

FIGURE 1 Benefits, barriers, and facilitating factors in advancing trauma-informed systems change.

trauma-sensitive services." Interviewees described the assessment process as invaluable to helping them to operationalize what it means to view service delivery systems and client experiences in court (or partner services) through a trauma lens. The phrase "Think trauma first" came up frequently in interviews as a phrase that helped individuals remember what they learned in the walk-throughs throughout their day-to-day practice. Further, many interviewees commented on the walk-throughs as being a catalyst for a general "culture change" in the community around implementing trauma-informed changes.

Benefits for clients. A common response regarding the benefits of implementing trauma-informed systems change is that service providers "have a higher level of sensitivity and respect for parents . . . in part, because of the trauma-informed trainings." The following quote also typifies comments made by interviewees:

> I look at what our parents go through and really try to put ourselves in their shoes and treat each other the way we want to be treated, but it also has this vibe of when we try to think about what we do and when we do it and why we do it the way . . . and it just makes us more aware of how we interact with our parents or how we talk to them or how we ask them to do things. I think the benefits would include that our parents get better services.

Respondents further related the success of trauma-based services and systems to the overall evidence supporting strengths-based approaches to service delivery, specifically highlighting the healing that can take place for parents and children alike when trauma is addressed at all levels of treatment:

> Not only are we thinking about the trauma of the parent and the child, but also we're steeped in the strength-based approach to recognizing that that parent knows their child best . . . and to improving ways to affirm that parent in their relationship with their child . . . and realizing that that can be one of the most healing experiences for the parent as well as the child. The two combined has been very powerful.

Generally speaking, most interviewees felt that the trauma-informed approach in FDTC made parents feel "heard" and "not judged." The parents were more likely to engage in the process and more likely to open up in the court setting. One interviewee commented, "I think that people are much more likely to be open and be willing to do what's necessary if they feel safe."

Benefits for service providers and systems. Benefits for service providers seemed to emerge around ideas of fostering "hope" and "inspiration." Although some staff discussed feeling stressed working in the field of child welfare, drug treatment, trauma, and the courts, respondents noted that trauma-informed systems change contributed to client success, which, in turn, directly affected their own job satisfaction. One respondent stated,

> I think it gets the parents comfortable with the team. It says, these are my allies, they're not my enemies, they're here to ensure success for me. . . . Because if they see that their court officer is paying attention to them, is interested in what they're saying, and is providing feedback, and if the team is providing feedback based on what they're saying, they become more interested. They buy into it, and they say, "Okay, well maybe this team does know what they're talking about." So I think those are some of the positive benefits. I mean, there's not a lot of wins in what we do, so it gives you little wins here and there . . . which give you energy and give you the inspiration and hope that you can keep doing it, because something good is coming from it.

Barriers to Implementing Trauma-Informed Systems Change

Respondents discussed a number of barriers to implementing trauma-informed systems change that were often related to barriers to systems change and collaboration in general. These barriers are described in the following four main areas: (a) physical, functional, and social context; (b) culture, philosophies, and values of different systems; (c) mandates of systems; and (d) systemic stressors.

Physical, functional, and social context. Themes emerged related to the physical, functional, and social environment of courts that are challenging for implementing trauma-informed systems change in court contexts. For instance, themes emerged describing the very purpose and history of the court system as one that is adversarial and confrontational in nature. The very experience of entering the courthouse can be triggering for clients. One interviewee from the domestic violence field stated, "What people experience coming into court, the huge challenges of the physical makeup of the building, in terms of the actual court process, it's overwhelming."

One participant reflected on the nature of the court as being a "foreign" and unfamiliar place for clients, and therefore, having the potential to be frightening:

> There was not a lot of room for confidential conversations, a lot of clients all mixed together. You get called by someone you don't know to come into the courtroom, and there are 10 people there. You might know your attorney and your social worker, but certainly the first time you walk in, you're walking into what's basically a foreign land, and it's not particularly welcoming.

Respondents also highlighted inherent triggers about the courts, such as security personnel, police guards, and metal detectors. One interviewee stated, "There are also criminal cases going on in the ground floor," indicating that parents and children appearing at dependency court are inherently going to be passing by individuals in prison garb and handcuffs, furthering feelings of being present in an unfriendly, unsafe environment.

Culture, philosophies, and values of different systems. "Different philosophical frameworks, different parameters in terms of ethical and legal obligations" inherent in the traditions and education of different disciplines and systems were noted by respondents as a significant barrier. For instance, many interviewees highlighted the differences in training and education of social workers, clinicians, and treatment providers to that of law enforcement, attorneys, and judges. Trauma-informed systems change, by nature, was described as conflicting with the training of professionals in the legal and law enforcement fields. One respondent wondered, "How do we get law enforcement on the bandwagon?" Others described issues with "the deputies and their attitudes and how they spoke to people." Respondents also described many challenges in working with attorneys who are trained differently than social workers. One respondent noted,

> Attorneys are trained, obviously, very differently . . . I mean, they're very humanistic, but they're attorneys, and it's a different role, so for me, the whole notion of trauma-based services . . . my problem interfacing with the attorneys is . . . they haven't worked with this vicarious trauma.

Other interviewees described barriers related to different value systems present in FDTCs, namely, values of the child welfare, substance abuse, and mental health systems. For example, one respondent commented on differing perceptions about efforts to implement trauma-informed systems changes and practices: "This is not enabling, not codependency. This is sensitivity to trauma survivors. . . . I think this comes from the lack of sensitivity about addiction." Many other respondents also described the difficulty service providers faced in stretching themselves beyond the traditional roles of their own system while practicing through a collaborative, trauma-informed lens.

Mandates of systems. Barriers related to legal mandates on systems were a common theme among participants in this study. In general, interviewees' responses reflected barriers related to "policies and procedures that will continue to exist always," that partners in the courts must follow and uphold that might or might not be trauma-informed.

One respondent expressed the difficult challenge of implementing trauma-informed systems change in a system that inherently causes additional trauma for both families and children. This interviewee stated:

> I think there has always been and continue to be a bit of a conflictual rub between making sure that the legal process and jurisprudence is adhered to and people are served in a client [centered], a trauma-informed way, and the legal process doesn't always facilitate that. And the child welfare process, very rarely do people feel good about removing children and about permanently removing children, and there's no way to make that a nontraumatic experience.

Similarly, some interviewees described tension around making the court safe versus making the court trauma-informed. Many interviewees seemed to struggle with that idea and expressed that that tension was a barrier.

> Deputies' obligation is to maintain safety in the court, not just in the courtroom, but throughout the courthouse. Their training is to take charge, to demonstrate that authority is necessary to maintain whatever needs to be maintained for safety, and sometimes that can be done in a very trauma sensitive way, but that's not where the deputies are coming from. And, sometimes if they used a trauma-informed approach, it might not be the right approach because of the circumstances. So, I think that there can be conversations, but we always have to loop back to what are the obligations?

Other responses highlighted legal mandates on the child welfare system and dependency courts that, at times, conflict with the pace of trauma treatment. This idea was exemplified by the observation that, "the court is time-limited, and not everybody can work on the court's clock . . . sometimes it's not reasonable to expect people can address these things in the period of time they have." Legal requirements related to case plans were also noted as a barrier to trauma-informed systems change. Whereas some respondents highlighted certain processes, such as family team meetings, which are geared toward making the case planning process more client-centered, others pointed to tensions around case planning in the context of systems that historically tended toward "cookie cutter" plans that were "lacking sensitivity" to individuals.

Systemic stressors. One final theme that emerged regarding barriers were system stressors inherently faced by social workers, clinicians, attorneys, judges, and all other professionals alike: "There are so many other demands." These stressors included high caseloads and limited funding, resources, and time. At the same time, some responses argued that the nature of trauma-informed systems change is not dependent on funding, typified by the following observation: "The minute you ask somebody to change they always say they need more funding, but you can do this very cheaply. You can really do this without a huge amount of additional funding."

Other barriers related to resources were frequent staff turnover and training opportunities. One respondent stressed the need for "ongoing discussions and ongoing training" due to the fact that "team members do change." Another interviewee stated, "We haven't had a consistent team, so that contributes to gaps."

Another prominent theme regarding stressors was the idea of vicarious trauma, described by most all interviewees as an enormous barrier to implementing trauma-informed change in court settings. One interviewee described vicarious trauma as a "systemic thing." Most interviewees acknowledged that not only are "clients regularly retraumatized over and over and over again by the system," but social workers and others working in the system are as well.

Facilitating factors to implementing trauma-informed systems change

Four major themes emerged related to facilitating factors to implementing trauma-informed systems change in the FDTC, which served to strengthen potential benefits and address barriers: (a) a formal commitment emphasizing ongoing training, walk-through assessments, and discussion about trauma-informed changes; (b) trauma leaders and champions; (c) support and advocacy through peer mentors; and (d) judicial leadership.

Formal commitment emphasizing ongoing training, walk-through assessments, and discussion about trauma-informed changes. Many respondents stressed the importance and helpfulness of sensing a formal commitment from leaders and partners in their systems toward making trauma-informed changes. This commitment was reflected in "ongoing conversations and honest sharing of concerns."

> We really need to implement that. Everyone has to take it on, every clinic manager, it has to start sort of at the top, with the executive management, senior management, at the management level. It used to be something that, to keep it alive you have to continuously raise it, raise its awareness. Discuss it.

One respondent commented on the role of upper management in implementing trauma-informed systems change with personnel who might have less education and training. "Supervisors are able to help the volunteers understand what it's like for a bio-parent to have so much trauma or a child to be part of our program." Many interviewees mentioned the various collaborative team meetings involved in FDTC, from management-level collaborative committees to teams involved in implementation, as particularly helpful in the collaboration aspect of implementing trauma-informed systems change.

Interviewees also reflected on the importance of always coming back to the table to discuss trauma-informed changes because of the time required to make these changes: "One [lesson] that we seem to have to learn over and over again is that it takes a long time to change systems. . . . The commitment has to be long term." Another interviewee emphasized that long-term commitment to training and ongoing discussion aids in bringing in new team members who might not be as familiar with trauma-informed services and systems. "Team members do change . . . and even for people who are experts, it never hurts to have a refresher and new discussion because you could always learn and think about things you've never thought about before." Other respondents emphasized the walk-through assessment process as a tool for both training and continued system improvements, including "Just checking and maybe doing periodic surveys, testing the knowledge and assessing all the different sites where there are clients."

Trauma leaders and champions. "It's extremely important that there are trauma champions. If you don't have the trauma champions, it's going to be very difficult." This and other comments describe the need for champions and leaders when implementing trauma-informed systems change. One respondent stressed the need to have multiple champions behind trauma-informed systems change because there is frequent staff turnover in the courts: "You never have just one champion within a system. You have to have a number." Other comments reflected the role that champions play in moving trauma-informed systems change along; for instance, "I think we need to have someone championing it. We need to have someone in the department who is taking this on and passing the word and going to meetings."

Support and advocacy through peer mentors. Interviewees frequently brought up the value of a peer support program (a key program component of the FDTC), which matches clients with mentor parents who are in recovery and have been through the child welfare system. "You just can't talk trauma-informed without having a [peer mentor] there," noted one interviewee. Another interviewee stated,

> I think the mentors are great as far as working with the parents, them sharing their story, and kind of giving them that encouragement to work, you know, whatever might be traumatizing . . . to think of other avenues that might be best for the child. . . . Mentors help talk the parent through what might be best for the child.

According to respondents, peer mentors not only help the parents walk through the court process, but also offer them hope. Peer mentors also provide important, needed insights to lawyers, social workers, other officials, and the judge in understanding what the parents go through as they navigate the system. One interviewee who served in a peer mentor role stated, "We were actually going to do a training for our agency about what we can do differently here from the mentors' perspectives." Peer mentors were frequently mentioned as key in implementing trauma-informed systems change because they are the window for the court into the trauma experience of parents and children in FDTCs.

Judicial leadership. One point made consistently across interviews was that of "bench leadership." One observation echoed across interviews was that the judge "made it clear from the very beginning that she thought this was important, that most people appearing [in the court] had trauma in their lives and that somehow the court had to address that and acknowledge it." Another interviewee also stated that the judge played an important role in explaining and educating the court about the effects of trauma on an individual's ability to parent:

> The judge went a long way to talk about the fact that most of the grown-ups had probably suffered the trauma, and that that would affect their ability to parent. . . . We have little impromptu meetings when there's some down time. The judge will say, "Well, what do you think about this? What do you think about that?" And I think that's where the judicial education is important, too, and getting feedback, consistently getting feedback, which will make it a better, it will make everyone feel like their voice is being heard and also maybe improvements can be made, and so I think that would be a great way to contribute to the whole, trauma-informed [systems change].

DISCUSSION

This study explored insights from key professionals working in the fields of substance abuse, mental health, child welfare, and the courts around their experience implementing trauma-informed systems change in a collaborative

FDTC setting. Results of the study describe the benefits and barriers to assessing and addressing the need for trauma-informed systems change in a collaborative context. Responses from key informers demonstrated the relevance of trauma-informed systems change in collaborative contexts, such as FDTCs, designed to address the complex needs of children and families.

Analysis of historical documents and interview narratives revealed a number of potential trauma "triggers" as well as strategies for reducing triggers, which might be relevant to practice across contexts (e.g., creating opportunities for client choice, rather than mandating specific treatment options). Findings from in-depth interviews underscore the importance of a wide variety of systems players (e.g., court, addiction services, child welfare, mental health) embracing a process of trauma-informed assessment and systems improvement in a planned, collaborative process that has as its core value to better address the needs of vulnerable families. The emphasis on development of shared values and adoption of specific system-level changes across systems is consistent with literature describing successful collaborative practice among dependency courts, child welfare, addiction treatment, and allied fields (Young & Gardner, 2002). Findings are also consistent with studies emphasizing the importance of strategic efforts for implementing system-wide changes in practice, engagement of multiple stakeholders, and shared governance (Elliott et al., 2005; Mildon & Shlonsky, 2011; Reed & Mazelis, 2005).

Study Limitations

This study has a number of limitations. Although this study obtained a sample of cross-systems partners and program representatives affiliated with one FDTC, the relatively small sample size of 12 interviewees limits the generalizability of the findings in other contexts. The sample included primarily leaders and other stakeholders who were highly involved in the FDTC and did not include a breadth of representatives from each partner system; consequently, findings might not be reflective of the perspectives of other leaders and line staff throughout different service delivery systems. Additional research would be needed to examine the degree to which trauma-informed systems change efforts penetrate and influence the perspectives and practices of leaders and providers throughout partner systems. In addition, purposive sampling was made possible with the help of key informants in the courts familiar with and integrated in trauma-informed systems change. Although historical documents were triangulated with interview data and a member-check process was implemented to strengthen trustworthiness and credibility of the findings, biases of the researchers and key informers have the potential to skew conclusions that can be drawn from this study.

CONCLUSION

This study demonstrates the impact of trauma-informed systems change initiatives in collaborative FDTCs and underscores the need for further inquiry and research in this area. In particular, there is a need for research documenting the implementation and outcomes of trauma-informed efforts in dependency court contexts, and other courts serving individuals with histories of trauma. There is also a need for research specifically examining outcomes for clients, particularly in regard to reunification and recovery, when courts are trauma-informed. Finally, it will be important that future research examine how addressing the issue of trauma among parents could impact children, particularly in children with histories of trauma, victimization, abuse, and removal from their parents. This future research will be particularly salient for understanding effective strategies at preparing children and families in the child welfare system for successful reunification.

Assessment tools, such as the trauma-informed systems walk-through, are important for organizational and service delivery improvement. They can demonstrate the impact of minimal cost activities on informing systems and services change. Cost-neutral or minimal-cost assessment processes have exceptional value in the human services field, especially considering the current fiscal climate, in identifying small, doable changes as a strategy for service improvement.

Collaborative process is a hallmark of social work practice. Advancing systems assessment processes and change efforts are valuable to fostering effective cross-systems collaboration, clarifying shared values, and developing a framework for congruent practice. According to Elliott et al. (2005), formal collaboration is especially critical in reducing trauma for consumers. FDTCs, in particular, interact with multiple systems players while addressing a multitude of complex problems, such as addiction, mental health, health, family violence, and child abuse. Therefore, implementing trauma-informed systems change in collaborative contexts, like FDTCs, has the potential for positive impact for practice, programming, and policy across these multiple systems. Finally, implementing trauma-informed systems change has the potential to greatly impact outcomes for clients, including their experience of different systems and faith in the recovery process.

REFERENCES

Amaro, H., Chernoff, M., Brown, V., Arévalo, S., & Gatz, M. (2007). Does integrated trauma-informed substance abuse treatment increase treatment retention? *Journal of Community Psychology*, *35*(7), 845–862.

Becker, M. A., Noether, C. D., Larson, M. J., Gatz, M., Brown, V., Heckman, J. P., & Giard, J. (2005). Characteristics of women engaged in treatment for trauma and co-occurring disorders: Findings from a national multisite study. *Journal of Community Psychology, 33*(4), 429–443.

Bloom, S. L. (2006). *Trauma-informed systems transformation: Recovery as a public health concern.* Philadelphia, PA: Trauma Task Force. Retrieved from http://www.sanctuaryweb.com/publications.php

Boles, S. M., Young, N. K., Moore, T., & DiPirro-Beard, S. (2007). The Sacramento dependency drug court: Development and outcomes. *Child Maltreatment, 12*(2), 161–171.

British Columbia Center of Excellence for Women's Health. (2011). *Coalescing on women and substance use: Assisting women with mental health, substance use and trauma-related concerns through trauma-informed approaches: Trauma-informed approaches online tool 1.0.* Retrieved from http://www.coalescing-vc.org/virtual Learning/documents/trauma-informed-online-tool.pdf

Brosky, B. A., & Lally, S. J. (2004). Prevalence of trauma, PTSD, and dissociation in court-referred adolescents. *Journal of Interpersonal Violence, 19*(7), 801–814.

Bryer, J., Nelson, B., Miller, J., & Krol, P. (1987). Childhood physical and sexual abuse as factors in adult psychiatric illness. *American Journal of Psychiatry, 144,* 1426–1430.

Buel, S. M. (2003). Addressing family violence within juvenile courts: Promising practices to improve intervention outcomes. *Journal of Aggression, Maltreatment, and Trauma, 8*(3), 273–307.

Carlson, B. E. (2006). Best practices in the treatment of substance-abusing women in the child welfare system. *Journal of Social Work Practice in the Addictions, 6*(3), 97–115.

Drabble, L. (2011). Advancing collaborative practice between substance abuse treatment and child welfare fields: What helps and hinders the process? *Administration in Social Work, 35*(1), 88–106.

Dube, S. R., Felitti, V. J., Dong, M., Giles, W. H., & Anda, R. F. (2003). The impact of adverse childhood experiences on health problems: Evidence from four birth cohorts dating back to 1900. *Preventative Medicine, 37,* 268–277.

Edwards, L. P., & Ray, J. A. (2005). Judicial perspectives on family drug treatment courts. *Juvenile and Family Court Journal, 56*(3), 1–27.

Elliott, D. E., Bjelajac, P., Fallot, R. D., Markoff, L. S., & Reed, B. G. (2005). Trauma-informed or trauma-denied: Principles and implementation of trauma-informed services for women. *Journal of Community Psychology, 33*(4), 429–443.

Fallot, R. D., & Harris, M. (2006). *Trauma-informed services: A self-assessment and planning protocol.* Washington, DC: Community Connections.

Felitti, V. J., Anda, R. F., Nordenberg, D., Williamson, D. F., Spitz, A. M., Edwards, V., . . . Marks J. S. (1998). Relationship of childhood abuse and household dysfunction to many of the leading causes of death in adults: The adverse childhood experiences (ACE) study. *American Journal of Preventative Medicine, 14*(4), 245–258.

Green, B. L., Furrer, C., Worcel, S., Burrus, S., & Finigan, M. W. (2007). How effective are family treatment drug courts? Outcomes from a four-site national study. *Child Maltreatment, 12*(1), 43–59. doi:10.1177/1077559506296317

Green, B. L., Rockhill, A., & Burrus, S. (2008). The role of interagency collaboration for substance-abusing families involved in child welfare. *Child Welfare, 87*(1), 29–61.

Green, B. L., Rockhill, A., & Furrer, C. (2006). Understanding patterns of substance abuse treatment for women involved with child welfare: The influence of the Adoption and Safe Families Act (ASFA). *The American Journal of Drug and Alcohol Abuse, 32*(2), 149–176. doi:10.1080/00952990500479282

Harris, M., & Fallot, R. (Eds.). (2001). *Using trauma theory to design service systems.* San Francisco, CA: Jossey-Bass.

Hodas, G. R. (2006). *Responding to childhood trauma: The promise and practice of trauma-informed care.* Harrisburg, PA: Pennsylvania Office of Mental Health and Substance Abuse Services. Retrieved from http://www.childrescuebill.org/VictimsOfAbuse/RespondingHodas.pdf

Kilpatrick, D., Acierno, R., Resnick, H., Saunders, B., & Best, C. (1997). A 2-year longitudinal analysis of the relationships between violence and substance abuse in women. *Journal of Consulting and Clinical Psychology, 65*, 834–857.

Ko, S. J., Ford, J. D., Kassam-Adams, N., Berkowitz, S. J., Wilson, C., Wong, M., . . . Layne, C. M. (2008). Creating trauma-informed systems: Child welfare, education, first responders, health care, juvenile justice. *Professional Psychology: Research and Practice, 39*(4), 396–404.

Lesperance, T., Moore, K. A., Barrett, B., Young, M. S., Clark, C., & Ochshorn, E. (2001). Relationship between trauma and risky behavior in substance abusing parents involved in family dependency treatment court. *Journal of Aggression, Maltreatment, and Trauma, 20*(2), 163–174. doi:10.1080/10926771.2011.546752

Marsh, J. C., Smith, B. D., & Bruni, M. (2010). Integrated substance abuse and child welfare services for women: A progress review. *Children and Youth Services Review, 33*(3), 466–472.

McHugo, G. J., Caspi, Y., Kamnierer, N., Mazelis, R., Jackson, E. W., Russell, L., . . . Kimerling, R. (2005). The assessment of trauma history in women with co-occurring substance abuse and mental disorders and a history of interpersonal violence. *Journal of Behavioral Health Services and Research, 32*(2), 113–127.

McHugo, G. J., Kammerer, N., Jackson, E. W., Markoff, L. S., Gatz, M., Larson, M. J., . . . Hennigan, K. (2005). Women, co-occurring disorders, and violence study: Evaluation design and study population. *Journal of Substance Abuse Treatment, 28*, 91–107.

Mildon, R., & Shlonsky, A. (2011). Bridge over troubled water: Using implementation science to facilitate effective services in child welfare. *Child Abuse & Neglect, 35*(9), 753–756.

Morrissey, J. P., Ellis, A. R., Gatz, M., Amaro, H., Reed, B. G., Savage, A., . . . Banks, S. (2005). Outcomes for women with co-occurring disorders and trauma: Program and person-level effects. *Journal of Substance Abuse Treatment, 28*, 121–133.

Morrissey, J. P., Jackson, E. W., Ellis, A. R., Amaro, H., Brown, V. B., & Najavits, L. M. (2005). Twelve-month outcomes of trauma-informed interventions for women with co-occurring disorders. *Psychiatric Services, 56*(10), 1213–1222.

Najavits, L. M., Weiss, R. D., & Shaw, S. R. (1997). The link between substance abuse and posttraumatic stress disorder in women: A research review. *American Journal on Addictions, 6*(4), 273–283.

National Association of State Mental Health Program Directors and National Technical Assistance Center for State Mental Health Planning. (2004). *The damaging consequences of violence and trauma: Facts, discussion points, and recommendations for the behavioral health system.* Washington, DC: U.S. Department of Health and Human Services.

National Center for Injury Prevention and Control. (2005a). *Child maltreatment: Overview.* Retrieved from www.cdc.gov/ncipc/factsheets/cmoverview.htm

National Center for Injury Prevention and Control. (2005b). *Child maltreatment: Prevention strategies.* Retrieved from www.cdc.gov/ncipc/factsheets/cmprevention.htm

Osterling, K. L., & Austin, M. J. (2008). Substance abuse interventions for parents involved in the child welfare system: Evidence and implications. *Journal of Evidence-Based Social Work, 5*(1/2), 157–189.

Reed, B., & Mazelis, R. (2005). Scholarship, collaboration, struggle, and learning in the women, co-occurring disorders, and violence study: Introduction to the 6-month outcome. *Journal of Substance Abuse Treatment, 28*, 87–89.

Ryan, J. P., Marsh, J. C., Testa, M. F., & Louderman, R. (2006). Integrating substance abuse treatment and child welfare services: Findings from the Illinois alcohol and other drug abuse waiver demonstration. *Social Work Research, 30*(2), 95–107.

Savage, A., Quiros, L., Dodd, S. J., & Bonavota, D. (2007). Building trauma-informed practice: Appreciating the impact of trauma in the lives of women with substance abuse and mental health problems. *Journal of Social Work Practice in the Addictions, 7*, 91–116.

Strauss, A. L. (1987). *Qualitative analysis for social services.* Cambridge, UK: Cambridge University Press.

Strauss, A. L., & Corbin, J. (1990). *Basics of qualitative research: Grounded theory procedures and techniques.* Newbury Park, CA: Sage.

Timko, C., & Moos, R. H. (2002). Symptom severity, amount of treatment, and 1-year outcomes among dual diagnosis patients. *Administration and Policy in Mental Health, 30*, 35–54.

U.S. Department of Health and Human Services. (1999). *Blending perspectives and building common ground: A report to Congress on substance abuse and child protection.* Washington, DC: U.S. Government Printing Office. Retrieved from aspe.hhs.gov/hsp/subabuse99/subabuse.htm

U.S. Department of Health and Human Services. (2010). *Targeted grants to increase the well-being of, and to improve the permanency outcomes for, children affected by methamphetamine or other substance abuse: First annual report to Congress.* Washington, DC: U.S. Department of Health and Human Services, Administration for Children and Families, Administration on Children, Youth and Families, Children's Bureau. Retreived from http://www.acf.hhs.gov/programs/cb/pubs/targeted_grants/targeted_grants.pdf

U.S. Department of Health and Human Services, Administration for Children and Families. (1997). *Adoption and Safe Families Act of 1997.* Retrieved from http://www.acf.hhs.gov/programs/cb/laws_policies/cblaws/public_law/p1105_89/p1105_89.htm

Worcel, S. D., Furrer, C. J., Green, B. L., Burrus, S. W. M., & Finigan, M. W. (2008). Effects of family treatment drug courts on substance abuse and child welfare outcomes. *Child Abuse Review, 17*(6), 427–443.

Young, N. K., Boles, S. M., & Otero, C. (2007). Parental substance use disorders and child maltreatment: Overlap, gaps, and opportunities. *Child Maltreatment, 12*(2), 137–149.

Young, N. K., & Gardner, S. (2002). *Navigating the pathways: Lessons and promising practices in linking alcohol and drug services with child welfare* (SAMHSA Pub. No. SMA-02-3639). Rockville, MD: Center for Substance Abuse Treatment, Substance Abuse and Mental Health Services Administration.

African American Adult Children of Alcoholics: An Interview With J. Camille Hall, PhD, LCSW

INTERVIEW CONDUCTED BY
LORI HOLLERAN STEIKER, PhD, ACSW
Associate Professor, School of Social Work, University of Texas at Austin, Austin, Texas, USA

One in eight Americans is an adult child of an alcoholic (ACoA; Grant, 2000). ACoA status puts such individuals at risk for a number of psychosocial difficulties: ACoAs have been found to be at increased risk for depression and alcohol abuse (LaBrie, Hummer, & Pederson, 2007), lower self-esteem than non-ACoAs (Geisner, Larimer, Neighbors, & Neighbors, 2004), and higher levels of college attrition (Kitsantas, Kitsantas, & Anagnostopoulou, 2008). Dr. J. Camille Hall has devoted her research to investigating the unique relationship between ethnicity and ACoA status, particularly among African American individuals. Dr. Hall is a 1991 and 1993 graduate of New Mexico State University (BSW, MSW) and Smith College (PhD). She is a licensed clinical social worker in New Mexico and Arkansas and has worked in private and public social service and mental health agencies as a clinical social worker for over 17 years. Dr. Hall is currently on the faculty at the University of Tennessee and continues to do research with ACoAs.

Holleran Steiker: To begin with, can you tell us about ACoAs and what brought you to study this aspect of social work?

Hall: Prior to working in academe, I was a clinician in the New Mexico Public Defender Department working as an alternative sentence planner, assessing and advocating for alternatives to incarceration for individuals based on criminal record, treatment history, and available resources. Previously, I also worked in Las Cruces, New Mexico, at a community action agency as a program administrator developing case management services for the homeless and indigent populations, and as a psychotherapist, utilizing cognitive-behavioral therapy to provide individual, group, and family therapy to adults, children, and geriatric clients. I also was a social worker with the New Mexico Children Youth and Families Department, conducting assessments of children and families related to child abuse and neglect. My curiosity began as a result of having encountered a number of clients who were children of alcoholics. I noticed that they had similar challenges and resources regardless of the setting and that some of them seemed to utilize the resources more efficiently than others. In addition, personally, my extended family members were instrumental in my successfully overcoming alcoholic parentage.

Holleran Steiker: Dr. Hall, I know many of our readers will identify and value your informed work. Can you give us an overview of what your research has indicated about African American children of addicts and alcoholics?

Hall: My recent research has focused on African American college students. In a study investigating how social support positively impacts how ACoAs cope, for instance, I found that this population uses more approach versus avoidant coping responses when compared to non-ACoAs; such an approach minimizes alcohol abuse (Hall, 2010). The data showed an interesting distinction by gender and ACoA status with regard to alcohol use—specifically, that African American males consumed more alcohol regardless of ACoA status. This finding countered the replicated study, which found that African American female ACoAs drank more than other groups (Rodney & Rodney, 1996). I have also investigated how multiple attachment bonds resulting from the African American cultural norm of having numerous kin and fictive kin (e.g., mentor, coach, teacher, play mothers and fathers) promote positive self-esteem, and increase satisfactory interpersonal relationships when compared to non-ACoAs. One study indicated that ACoAs' family communication and social support are particularly protective. African American ACoAs with the support of kin or fictive kin (i.e., those who serve in roles as if they were family) were clearly more resilient than those without such supports (Hall, 2008, 2013). In addition, my work has shown that higher social class, social support, and a stable family environment lend themselves to higher levels of resilience as well (see Hall, 2007).

Holleran Steiker: What, in summary, would you say is the most important thing that you have learned from research about cultural factors that contribute to the functioning of ACoAs as children and adults?

Hall: Although some of my work supports previous findings (e.g., social support and family communication as protective factors), other findings highlight the fact that ACoAs are not, in fact, a homogenous group and do not necessarily conform to the popular literature's symptoms and categories (Hall, 2007, 2008, 2010).

Holleran Steiker: Can you explain the existing efforts, settings, unmet needs, and related challenges with regard to addicted families and ACoAs?

Hall: More work needs to be pursued with regard to understanding the importance of culturally relevant factors that promote resilience, such as social support. We must continue to explore the value of attachment bonds, which increase survivability and resilience of children at risk. New directions have been pursued in ACoA research and intervention due to new insights and technologies. For example, there are a growing number of web-based and computer-based interventions for children of alcoholics (e.g., see Elgán, Hansson, Zetterlind, Kartengren, & Leifman, 2012; Gustafson, McTavish, Schubert, & Johnson, 2012).

Holleran Steiker: What surprises have you encountered in your research?

Hall: My work shows that African Americans are more likely than Caucasians to live in extended family situations with varied forms of social support. This did not surprise me. However, I have witnessed that the fictive kin phenomena is most often cross-cultural; the majority of the research participants indicated that their tangible support was provided by people not of color. Many of the female ACoAs stated that emotional support was vital to their survival and they routinely sought "objective" feedback from fictive kin, who were mainly people not of color. I am not sure if this related to urban versus rural settings or resource issues, but this trend is unlike any other I have seen and it definitely warrants future research and exploration.

Holleran Steiker: What are your visions for behavioral health research and interventions that might grow from your work in the future?

Hall: Utilization of culturally responsive interventions. Hopefully, clinicians will realize the value in "strengths"-based assessment of clients and specifically their family members. Especially within the rubric of the social work knowledge base, it is critical that we move toward an understanding of the importance of social support, including the tangible and nontangible forms to enhance coping responses for this population. I also think it is important to continue research that will investigate preventive measures. We need techniques that will help ACoAs develop positive self-esteem and satisfactory interpersonal relationships. In addition, developing evidence-based models that focus on how social support can sometimes improve ACoAs' resiliency, coping, and self-esteem, especially in the case of Black women.

Holleran Steiker: What recommendations can you make to social workers who want to pursue this area of research or interventions with ACoAs, especially those of color?

Hall: I recommend that social work researchers explore predictive factors that will lead to the development of evidence-based practice models with this population. Most important, I strongly encourage all practitioners and educators to utilize and stress the necessity of ethnic sensitive service delivery.

Holleran Steiker: Can our readers contact you if they would like to learn more? If so, what is the best way to reach you?

Hall: I am happy to hear from readers with comments or questions. It is best to reach me at this e-mail address: Jha1139@utk.edu.

REFERENCES

Elgán, T. H., Hansson, H., Zetterlind, U., Kartengren, N., & Leifman, H. (2012). Design of a web-based individual coping and alcohol-intervention program (web-ICAIP) for children of parents with alcohol problems: Study protocol for a randomized controlled trial. *BMC Public Health, 16*, 12–35.

Geisner, I. M., Larimer, M. E., Neighbors, C., & Neighbors, C. (2004). The relationship among alcohol use, related problems, and symptoms of psychological distress. *Addictive Behaviors, 6*, 843–848.

Grant, B. F. (2000). Estimates of U.S. children exposed to alcohol abuse and dependence in the family. *American Journal of Public Health, 90*, 112–126.

Gustafson, D. H., McTavish, F. M., Schubert, C. J., & Johnson, R. A. (2012). The effect of a computer-based intervention on adult children of alcoholics. *Journal of Addictive Medicine, 6*(1), 24–28.

Hall, J. C. (2007). An exploratory study of the role of kinship ties in promoting resilience among African American adult children of alcoholics. *Journal of Human Behavior in the Social Environment, 15*(2), 61–78.

Hall, J. C. (2008). The impact of kin and fictive kin relationships on the mental health of Black adult children of alcoholics. *Health & Social Work, 33*(4), 259–266.

Hall, J. C. (2010). Childhood perceptions of family, social support, parental alcoholism and later alcohol use among African American college students. *Journal of Substance Use, 15*(3), 157–165.

Hall, J. C. (2013). Resilience despite risk: Understanding African-American ACoAs kin and fictive kin relationships. In D. S. Becvar (Ed.), *Handbook of family resilience* (pp. 481–494, Part 6). New York, NY: Springer.

Kitsantas, P., Kitsantas, A., & Anagnostopoulou, T. (2008). A cross-cultural investigation of college student consumption: A classification tree analysis. *Journal of Psychology, 14*, 5–11.

LaBrie, J. W., Hummer, J. F., & Pederson, E. R. (2007). Reasons for drinking in the college student context: The differential role and risk of the social motivator. *Journal of Studies of Alcohol & Drugs, 68*, 393–398.

Rodney, H. E., & Rodney, L. (1996). An exploratory study of African American collegiate adult children of alcoholics. *Journal of American College Health, 44*(6), 267–272.

ENDPAGE

Mentalization-Based Treatment: A Valuable Framework for Helping Maltreating Parents

CHRISTINE H. FEWELL, PhD

Adjunct Professor, Silver School of Social Work, New York University, New York, New York, USA

In a study of the effects of parental alcoholism on college students at a large Northeastern urban university (Fewell, 2006), a 20-year-old student answered a question about why she thought her mother and father acted the way they did during her childhood and what effect it had on who she is today by saying the following:

> My father drank a lot and also had a very bad temper. He would hit my brother all the time. I would just sit in the corner in silence and not know what to think. I was terrified, but not hit by my father, just by my mother. He would scream at my mother all the time. There was constant screaming in my house. I don't know who was louder, my father or my mother. I was just terrified. I grew up in total fear. My mother hated when my father drank. He would get so crazy. It was unbearable. I hated it. I think because of him I fell in love with a lot of people with uncontrollable tempers who have massive issues. It is just horrible.

Her description of the parents' conflicts and inability to think about the mind of their child and how to help soothe her terror are evident. This vignette shows how substance abuse impairs mentalizing not only in the person who abuses substances, but also frequently in the partner who is preoccupied with the other's substance abuse.

Mentalizing involves the ability to imagine what might be on another's mind and the ability to perceive and interpret human behavior in terms of intentional mental states. It involves the capacity to think about others' needs, desires, feelings, beliefs, goals, purposes, and reasons. The ability to mentalize helps us predict, explain, and justify the actions of others by inferring the intentional mental states that cause them (Allen & Fonagy, 2006). This permits one to regulate affect and choose a modulated response that takes into account the minds of others instead of overreacting to a perceived insult or behavior. The ability to mentalize is acquired within the context of a secure child–adult attachment relationship in which caretakers are able to reflect back to the child an understanding of his or her feelings and state of mind. At the other end of the spectrum, people who have experienced attachment trauma as a result of being maltreated as a child live in a state of chronic activation of high levels of arousal and fear of exploring the minds of others (Fonagy, 2008). They are vulnerable to using drugs and alcohol as a way to self-soothe this chronic hyperarousal, as well as unable as parents to contemplate the mental states of their children apart from their own state of mind (Flores, 2004).

Recently, mentalization-based treatment (MBT) has been developed for use with a variety of client groups (Bateman & Fonagy, 2007; Fearon et al., 2006). Mentalizing interventions are conceived as a way to help clients develop skills that will enable them to regulate their affect in times of high emotional arousal. Helping parents to develop the ability to mentalize about their children aids in stopping the intergenerational perpetuation of insecure attachment and resulting maltreatment (Weinfield, Sroufe, & Egeland, 2000).

Facilitating the ability of parents to mentalize about the minds of their babies has been found to result in positive outcomes for high-risk young mothers (Sandler, Slade, & Mayes, 2006). Called "Minding the Baby," this Yale University–based research study works with high-risk, first-time adolescent mothers living in poverty in New Haven, CT. A multidisciplinary team, including a pediatric nurse and a social worker, makes home visits to the young woman during pregnancy and continues doing so through the second birthday of the child. Concrete services are provided to form a relationship. Through the use of a secure attachment relationship with the team, the mother is helped to learn to acknowledge, label, and tolerate mental states in herself and her baby. Preliminary research has demonstrated positive results.

Another reflective parenting program designed at Yale Child Study Center called Parents First (Goyette-Ewing et al., 2002) consists of a 12-week group intervention for use in educational and child care settings for parents of infants, toddlers, and preschoolers. Progressively more reflective exercises are used during group sessions, while the parents participate in simple family activities between sessions. The staff models reflectiveness by showing curiosity about how the child is feeling and what the child is thinking, and asks questions to promote parents' thinking about the child's mind.

Another program studied at Yale is the Mothers and Toddlers program for substance-using mothers with young children from birth to 3 years old who are attending an outpatient drug treatment program (Suchman, Decoste, Rosenberger, & Mcmahon, 2012). The goal is to help mothers increase their maternal reflective function so that they can understand their own and their children's intentions within a developmental framework. Such techniques as demonstrating curiosity about the baby's mind ("What is the baby thinking?"), or speaking for the baby by giving the baby a voice to demonstrate another point of view, are part of the manual-guided, 12-session, weekly individual therapy protocol. In addition, the Anna Freud Centre in London is continuing to develop and offer short term MBT to families (MBT–F) to help them learn the skill of mentalizing. Many protocols and background information, including YouTube video role-play demonstrations of various interventions to increase mentalizing capacity, are available and downloadable at mbtf.tiddlyspace.com.

The famous Adverse Childhood Experiences study found that 23.5% of respondents reported being exposed to family alcohol abuse and 4.9% reported family drug abuse (Anda et al., 2006). Even in this low-risk, middle-class sample, adverse childhood experiences were found to predict significant negative health consequences, as well as significant negative emotional consequences, including alcohol and drug abuse, or marrying someone who has alcohol or drug abuse problems, thus perpetuating the cycle. Mentalization-based interventions offer the possibility of intervening in the negative cycle of intergenerational attachment trauma to provide both the maltreating substance-using parent and their children a means for developing the essential skills for self-regulation, ultimately becoming better parents.

REFERENCES

Allen, J. G., & Fonagy, P. (2006). *Handbook of mentalization-based treatment*. Chichester, UK: Wiley.

Anda, R., Felitti, V., Bremner, J., Walker, J., Whitfield, C., Perry, B., . . . Giles, W. H. (2006). The enduring effects of abuse and related adverse experiences in childhood. *European Archives of Psychiatry and Clinical Neuroscience, 256*, 174–186.

Bateman, A. W., & Fonagy, P. (2007). *Mentalization-based treatment for borderline personality disorder: A practical guide*. Oxford, UK: Oxford University Press.

Fearon, P., Target, M., Sargent, J., Williams, L., McGregor, J., Bleiberg, E., & Fonagy, P. (2006). Short-term mentalization and relational therapy (SMART): An integrative family therapy for children and adolescents. In J. G. Allen & P. Fonagy (Eds.), *Handbook of mentalization-based treatment* (pp. 201–222). Chichester, UK: Wiley.

Fewell, C. H. (2006). *Attachment, reflective function, family dysfunction and psychological distress in college students with alcoholic parents* (Unpublished doctoral dissertation). New York University School of Social Work, New York, NY.

Flores, P. (2004). *Addiction as an attachment disorder*. New York, NY: Aronson.

Fonagy, P. (2008). The mentalization-focused aproach to social development. In F. N. Busch (Ed.), *Mentalization: Theoretical considerations, research findings, and clinical implications* (pp. 3–56). New York, NY: The Analytic Press.

Goyette-Ewing, M., Slade, A., Knoebber, K., Gilliam, W., Truman, S., & Mayes, L. (2002). *Parents First: A developmental parenting program*. Unpublished manuscript, Yale Child Study Center, New Haven, CT.

Sandler, L. S., Slade, A., & Mayes, L. C. (2006). Minding the baby: A mentalization-based parenting program. In J. G. Allen & P. Fonagy (Eds.), *Handbook of mentalization-based treatment* (pp. 271–288). Chichester, UK: Wiley.

Suchman, N., Decoste, C., Rosenberger, P., & Mcmahon, T. (2012). Attachment-based intervention for substance-abusing mothers: A preliminary test of the proposed mechanisms of change. *Infant Mental Health Journal*, *33*(4), 360–371.

Weinfield, N. S., Sroufe, A., & Egeland, B. (2000). Attachment from infancy to adulthood in a high risk sample. Continuity, discontinuity, and their correlates. *Child Development*, *71*, 695–702.

Index

Page numbers in *italics* indicate tables.